# CROSSCURRENTS
PURSUING SOCIAL JUSTICE AND INTERRELIGIOUS WORK
SINCE 1950

*CrossCurrents* (ISSN 0011-1953; online ISSN 1939-3881) connects the wisdom of the heart with the life of the mind and the experiences of the body. The journal is operated through its parent organization, the Association for Public Religion and Intellectual Life (APRIL), an interreligious network of academics, activists, artists, and community leaders seeking to engage the many ways religion meets the public. Contributions to the journal exist at the nexus of religion, education, the arts, and social justice. The journal is published quarterly on behalf of the Association for Public Religion and Intellectual Life by the University of North Carolina Press.

The Association for Public Religion and Intellectual Life (formerly ARIL) is a global network of leaders, scholars, and social change agents who explore religious life, engage in intellectual inquiry, and lead ethical action in the world today. Their primary objective, especially through annual summer colloquia and *CrossCurrents*, is to bring together leading voices of our time to advocate for justice and to examine global spiritual and interreligious currents in both historical and contemporary perspectives.

A membership to APRIL includes access to *CrossCurrents* starting with Volume 58, 2008, though our partners at Project MUSE, monthly newsletters, early access to summer colloquium themes, a 40% on UNC Press books, and more. For more information, including membership and subscription rates, visit www.aprilonline.org.

This reissue of *CrossCurrents* was one of four issues published in 2019 as part of Volume 69. For a current masthead visit www.aprilonline.org.

© 2019 Association for Public Religion and Intellectual Life. All rights reserved.

ISBN 978-1-4696-6719-5 (Print)

I0272135

# CROSSCURRENTS

## THE CURRENT AND FUTURE DIRECTIONS OF THEOLOGICAL EDUCATION

Edited by Christian Scharen

5
*The Current and Future Directions of Theological Education*
**Christian Scharen**

10
*Liberating and Diversifying Theological Education: A Subversive or Empowering Aspiration?*
**Amos Yong**

18
*Buy a Field: The Future of Theological Educators*
**Willie James Jennings**

24
*From Multiculturality to Interculturality: The Aim of Theological Education in Today's Global Context*
**vănThanh Nguyễn**

29
*No Joke! Resisting the "Culture of Disbelief" that Keeps Clergy Women Pushing Uphill*
**Eileen R. Campbell-Reed**

39
*The Telos of Theological Education: A Theological Reflection*
**Scott Woodward**

45
*Teaching Other Faiths About Islam: A Transformative Journey*
**Zainab Alwani**

59
*"Knowing Who," A Sermon on Proverbs 8:1-21*
**Ted A. Smith**

**64**
*Teaching Toward the Practice of Ministry Today*
**Christian Scharen**

**74**
*Identity Quests, Indebted Diversities, and Serving "The Church":*
*Living the Questions of Ministerial Formation*
**C. Melissa Snarr**

**80**
*Why Games and Gaming Might be the Best Way and Place in Which to Consider the*
*Meaning and Purposes of Theological Education: A Reflection*
**Mary E. Hess**

**95**
*Notes on Contributors*

About the Cover: Cover photo used with permission of iStock photos at Getty Images.

## CROSSCURRENTS

# THE CURRENT AND FUTURE DIRECTIONS OF THEOLOGICAL EDUCATION

Christian Scharen

Discussions of the "current and future directions of theological education" in the United States too often center on the story and circumstances of historically white Protestant theological schools. A case in point is the recent spate of articles on Andover Newton, the oldest free-standing theological school in the United States, closing its Boston campus and embedding at Yale alongside their divinity school.[1] Auburn Seminary's Center for the Study of Theological Education has always held a wider view. Writing in its founding charter, my predecessor, Barbara Wheeler and her colleague Linda-Marie Delloff wrote that "theological education is not restricted to theological schools," and "is less a single enterprise than it is a network of allied enterprises that, beneath some common features, have many important differences."[2] More recently, Justo Gonzalez aptly put it this way: Theological education is not merely a higher education degree earned in a theological school, but a broad "continuum" of practices extending from childhood to old age, inclusive of many different informal and formal settings.[3]

Further adding to the challenge of describing the "current and future directions of theological education," such efforts emerge from the tumult of this moment when changes in the nation's demographics and modes of religious belief and practice are undergoing dramatic change. Many of the historical white Protestant theological schools, as well as mainstream Catholic and Evangelical ones, are adapting to declining enrollment, mirroring their partner churches' decline in membership, even as new immigrant populations—and their new initiatives in theological education—are growing rapidly. In short, these dramatic changes portend a radical decentering from the presumed center of theological education, opening up a new geography representing contested stories and spaces for theological education in, and quite far beyond, the traditional seminary or theological school.

Theological education literature is overdue in its coming to terms with a new contested geography. A step toward more adequate mapping of the ecology of theological education must start with the United States' twin original sins, Native genocide and African slavery. New narrations of theological education ought to start with such facts as the use of the 15th-century medieval papal "doctrine of discovery" that legitimized—in God's name—the dehumanization, destruction, and enslavement of other humans for the creation of wealth for European nations.[4] Early post-colonial scholar Aimé Césaire put it bluntly: "colonization = 'thingification'." "Between colonizer and colonized there is only room for forced labor, intimidation, pressure, the police, taxation, theft, rape, compulsory crops, contempt, mistrust, arrogance, self-complacency, swinishness, brainless elites, degraded masses."[5] While different in degree and form of impact, these forces bore and continue to bear down on all black and brown people, those of Latinx and Asian descent, as well. The "theological education" allowing for such cultural—and eventual racial—supremacy, according to the landmark work of J. Kameron Carter, has its theological origins in an early decisive split between Christianity and Judaism, a split that allowed Christianity to cordon itself off as a racial religion of non-Jews.[6]

This legacy of European theological education formed and funded the assault of European global imperialism. As Chickasaw theologian Lisa Dellinger shows, they made effective use of a doctrine of sin that labeled all dark-skinned peoples as "savages, child-like, devils, uncivilized, interior, animals, doomed, and worthy only of death."[7] One could imagine taking this starting place and doing a history of theological education from the missions of California and the Southwest, from the early forts of the French traders in their encounters with Natives in the upper Great Lakes region, or from the brush arbor of Southern plantation life. One could investigate the role of pastors assigned to Japanese internment camps during World War II, or the role of Roman Catholics religious in running many of the Native American boarding schools. Today, such efforts would investigate Underground Seminary in Minneapolis with its intentionally anti-empire curriculum and pedagogy, or to Howard University Divinity School with its deep commitments to theological education in the prisons, fighting mass incarceration from the inside, or to the thousands of Hispanic Bible Institutes like Calvario City Church in Orlando, FL, a loose network of Latinx formation for Christian life and leadership open to all regardless of typical academic credentials (a bachelor's degree) required of most traditional seminaries, among others.

These essays, emerging at the intersection of multiple new projects investigating the current shape of theological education, begin very much with stories told as critique, with a focus on liberation, and serious engagement with intersectional oppression along the issues of race/ethnicity, gender, class, sexuality, educational status, and more. Amos Yong, in a very personal and reflective essay, takes on the exclusionary consequences of the pervasive white, middle-class assumptions of dominant forms of theological education embodied in most theological schools. Willie James Jennings highlights the ways these same normative white male assumptions and institutional practices reproduce this unjust system through the particular workings of the doctoral preparation and support for faculty members, especially as it impacts minoritized scholars. vanThan Nguyen offers a nuanced take, via the biblical example of Saul/Paul of Tarsus, for moving from a model of a white-hosted multicultural table without the practice of shared power and reciprocity, to an intercultural table with intentionality about practicing shared power and reciprocity, and the importance of this for the kind of nation and world we live in now. Finally, Eileen Campbell-Reed takes on the persistent presence of sexism and misogyny present in theological education and ministry, both taking stock of progress and the long journey yet to go in achieving real parity between men and women.

Additional essays expand these themes of liberation and critique of the normative white European Christian form of much of theological education, taking up the realities of a newly visible pluralism, a diversity rooted in subaltern populations that have in fact been present in the United States all along, but for various reasons now are more readily seen fully. Scott Woodward offers a dramatic case study in the globalizing and ecumenizing character of Roman Catholic theological education in the

United States and some of the profound impacts of this for how one even imagines theological education. Zainab Alwani offers an equally striking case study of the impact of teaching Islam and interfaith engagement in a predominately Christian divinity school at a time of gross misunderstanding of and hostility toward the Islamic tradition. Muslims have been in the United States since its beginning, she argues, including significant numbers of African slaves.[8]

Another way into alternative descriptions of the geography of theological education is to highlight the particular kinds of wisdom entailed in spiritual formation, wisdom increasingly being sought and found in contexts outside of traditional schools and classrooms, and with vocational goals beyond more traditional professional ministry leadership roles. Ted Smith articulates, via the genre of a sermon, how the traditional modes of knowledge assumed by the academy, while important, are not neither enough nor the central, defining type of knowledge at the heart of spiritual experience. Christian Scharen's research describes the ways in which such knowledge—what he calls "pastoral imagination"—is gained through immersion in contexts of practice. This phronetic capacity offers just the kind of dynamic ability to discern and decide paths of action in a time of rapid change when questions and curiosity seem the necessary leadership qualities rather than answers and certainty about the right path.

Lastly, major shifts in affiliation to traditional religious communities and practices, especially among the millennial generation (who report higher that 40% unaffiliated with any particular religious group), lead both to a wider interest in spirituality and kinds of gatherings and practices of connection and meaning, as well as much wider and more diverse vocational intentions than leadership of religious congregations. C. Melissa Snarr reflects on the ways these dynamics are present at a historic university-related divinity school, reporting on the connections between young people's experience of religiously inflicted wounds, striking diversity, broadening vocations, and a desire for living questions, all of which dominates the life of the school. Mary Hess, working at the intersection of a traditional mainline Protestant denominational seminary and cultures of community and practice outside of religious communities, raises fascinating questions about the formative impact of the new culture of technology, media, globalization, and the Internet, taking particular account of gaming culture as an alternative space of gathering and meaning-making more traditional religious communities might learn from.

This issue is intended to be more provocative than definitive, and not merely as a matter of noting practical limits but rather offered as an assertion. Part of the dynamic a liberative approach requires is a carnivalesque reversal of the dominate white male European hold on theological education's imagination, stepping to the side and joining a robustly contested space of difference and multiple stories whose voices now constitute the current and future shape of theological education.

I give thanks to two projects in theological education that informed this issue. First is a project based at Emory University's Candler School of Theology, Theological Education Between the Times, under the direction of Ted A. Smith, and funded by The Lilly Endowment. The second is a project based at Lancaster Theological Seminary, The Current and Future Directions of Theological Education, under the co-direction of David Mellot and Deborah F. Mullen, and funded by the Henry Luce Foundation.

**Notes**
1. https://religionnews.com/2015/11/13/oldest-u-s-graduate-seminary-to-close-campus-denominations-secularization-andover-theological/; https://www.insidehighered.com/quicktakes/2017/07/21/andover-newton-finalizes-plan-move-yale.
2. Barbara G. Wheeler and Linda-Marie Delloff, *Reaching Out: Auburn Seminary Launches the Center for the Study of Theological Education*, Auburn Studies Summer 1993, 8.
3. Justo Gonzalez, *A Brief History of Theological* Education (Nashville, TN: Abington Press, 2015), p. 42.
4. Robert Miller, Jacinta Ruru, Larissa Behrendt, and Tracy Linberg, Discovering Indigenous Lands: The Doctrine of Discovery in the English Colonies (New York, NY: Oxford, 2012).
5. Aimé Césaire, *Discourse on Colonialism*, trans. Joan Pinkham (New York, NY: Monthly Review Press, 1972), p. 42.
6. J. Kameron Carter, *Race: A Theological Account* (New York, NY: Oxford, 2008), p. 4. See also Willie James Jennings, *The Christian Imagination: Theology and the Origins of Race* (New Haven, CT: Yale University Press, 2011).
7. Lisa Dellinger, Ambiguity, Complexity, and the Sin of Nonconforming," 126 in Steven Charleston and Elaine Robinson, eds. Coming Full Circle: Constructing Native Christian Theology (Minneapolis, MN: Fortress Press, 2015).
8. https://nmaahc.si.edu/explore/stories/collection/african-muslims-early-america

# CROSSCURRENTS

# LIBERATING AND DIVERSIFYING THEOLOGICAL EDUCATION
A Subversive or Empowering Aspiration?

Amos Yong

Historic institutions of theological education are struggling amidst the vulnerability and fragility that characterizes much of the higher educational enterprise. As a (practically[1]) tenured professor, however, I wonder to what degree such job security actually undermines rather than empowers my envisioning and then working toward a liberating theological education that can engage the opportunities and challenges of the twenty-first century. Perhaps the underlying issue concerns whether theological education needs liberation in the present time and if so, from what, and what that means. To place the questions squarely on the table, I need to be honestly self-reflective about issues related to diversity and context and perhaps enter into the vulnerability that assails the wider theological guild.

I begin by reflecting about my recent visit to New York Theological Seminary (NYTS) just a week after the announcement (December 3, 2014) that the Staten Island grand jury had declined to indict the police officer under whose grip it appeared that Eric Garner had died (July 17, 2014). In part related to the release of my new book on Asian American evangelicalism in November of this year,[2] my longtime friend and NYTS associate professor Peter Heltzel had invited me to address the NYTS community about issues of race and ethnicity. In the wake of the unrest related to the announcement, as well as the wider national issues related to police brutality and race relations (e.g., the Michael Brown case in Ferguson, Missouri), Peter continually urged me to press into issues regarding social justice and racial reconciliation from my Asian American evangelical location.

Late Thursday, December 11, after having spent the afternoon and evening in discussion with NYTS faculty, staff, students, and others, Peter checked me into one of the Landmark guest rooms at Union Theological Seminary (kiddie-corner from NYTS). A few minutes after he left, I heard a hurried knock on my door: Peter insisted that I needed to accompany him to join a rally a few blocks away. It was about 10 PM, I was almost in bed, and the temperature was in the low 30s Fahrenheit, as I recall. But Peter was persistent: I could not be in a hotel room in the City that night while things he cared so much about were unfolding down the street.

Here, I have to digress and say a few words about Peter. Having grown up in Mississippi, he has been attuned to racial tensions from a young age. Although trained classically as a systematic theologian, since his arrival at NYTS almost ten years ago (at time of writing), he has been working intentionally at the intersection of racial reconciliation and social justice.[3] But Peter is no armchair theologian. Deftly deploying his social and political capital as a white male anti-racist/pro-reconciliation ally with people of color and following the black leadership of the #BlackLivesMatter Movement, Peter has facilitated strategic dialogues, written op-eds, helped organize rallies, participated in protests and marches, mobilized activists, advocated to politicians, and worked collaboratively as a faith-rooted organizer across racial, class, gender, and religious lines.

Along the way, Peter founded the Micah Institute, which mission, "[i]nspired by the Hebrew prophet Micah's call to act justly, love mercy and walk humbly with God, [is] to inspire and educate faith leaders to fight poverty and injustice" (see http://www.nyts.edu/the-micah-institute/). The Micah Institute's work is guided by a faith-rooted organizing, gathering people for social change shaped by the deepest wells of their faith traditions. In contrast to the instrumental approach of national organizing networks in the Alinsky tradition, faith-rooted organizing mobilizes public resistance, while treating all God's children with love and respect.[4] Over the last decade, Peter has emerged as a public theologian and activist in New York City, thereby not only retrieving but also transforming and extending the legacies of Reinhold Niebuhr and Paul Tillich through boldly confronting the "powers and principalities" of systemic racism as an anti-racist leader in the growing movement for a prophetic, intercultural future in our racially charged North American context of the third millennium.

I was reluctant to join Peter, especially considering that, by his own confession, it was not being thrown in jail for his activism that he was concerned about (in fact, that would be ideal for calling attention to the things he was committed to), but that he realized his efforts proceeded with great personal risk. Plus, not only was I not a New Yorker, but I would be a yellow person in a black-and-white world, and rallies, protests, and marches were not on my resume. But I realized that my deep friendship with Peter (we had gone to graduate school together) left me no alternative: I *needed* to be with him on this occasion, so I braved the elements, walked the streets of Upper Manhattan, and got to feel, if only for a few moments, what my friend has long been passionate about.

We jumped in a cab with a Union Theological Seminary student and a Ferguson Freedom fighter, who gave us an analysis of the goals of the #BlackLivesMatter movement as an anti-racist social movement (vs. conventional political movement) on our way down to the protest. When we arrived an African American speaker was chanting "I can't breathe, I can't breath!" as a testimony to the life of Eric Garner and calling on the crowd to join the "Justice for All" march on Washington, DC, scheduled for that weekend, on Saturday, December 13. I was able to meet Cornel West and other activists, and for a moment experienced the feeling of deep solidarity in the movement for racial and economic justice that is Peter's daily reality as an activist theologian in New York City.

I recount this experience because my more recent work not just as a Pentecostal or Evangelical but as an Asian America theologian has led me to ask questions about race, ethnicity, and justice in theological education.[5] Thinking about the future of theological education at this juncture, and with memories of my visit to NYTS, challenges me on multiple fronts. It is not just that my theologian friend practices what he preaches, even if that is more than sufficient to register existential *angst* in my own soul given the platforms to speak and preach that have been open to me. Further, it is not just that NYTS and its Micah Institute are engaging seminarians in important theological, socio-political, and practical matters,[6] although that also should sound notes for urgency for theological educators who realize that such will be central to the evolving urban contexts for ministry and mission in the twenty-first century.

More personally and troublingly for me is that Peter's commitments and *modus operandi* as a theologian and theological educator interrogate the deep structure of the theological academy as such as emerged over the last century. To put it bluntly, theological education as it persists today is a deeply white and middle-class endeavor, and the intertwined issues of racial reconciliation and social justice are dissonant within this academic context. Things are further complexified for Asian American scholars and theologians like me who exist liminally between "black" and "white" as (putatively) both "model minority" and "perpetual foreigner."[7] Let me further unpack such a conundrum from three sets of perspectives: that of faculty, that of students, and that of the churches which seminaries seek to serve.

First, faculty themselves, with the Ph.D. (required by almost all ATS-affiliated institutions), are a very privileged group of people. Yet not only does my very high level of education remove me from where most people live, what it takes to advance as a faculty member—scholarship and publications, to be direct—requires the kind of leisure (for research, reflection, and writing) that most people cannot afford. We have all been socialized to believe that earning the Ph.D. gives us the right to think and talk publicly about the subject matter that is our area of expertise, but it is precisely such cerebral activity, highly rewarded for academics, that works against our efforts to be liberative educators.

The reason is that our pursuit of the life of the mind removes us from the more pressing realities of daily life experienced by the poor, the oppressed, and the marginalized, especially people of color.[8] So if faculty members can only teach what they know and lead where they have been,[9] then we Ph.D.s might be very good at developing other Ph.D.s, but we will be much less adept, as I painfully felt on the streets of Manhattan that night, at teaching about and leading the charge toward a transformative and liberative theological education for those who remain outside the middle-class orbit. And if that is the case, then we have to be much more intentionally focused on being in solidarity with others who exist under much different circumstances and constraints than we do just so that we can have a chance to imagine, and then enact, a theological education that can be liberative for a diverse and conflicted world. But this begs the question: Does the liberation of others consist in becoming a middle-class consumer like me? As an Asian American, this forces me to face up to the upward social mobility expected of those classified as "yellow" even as it presses the question of what responsibilities the educationally privileged have and how they (we) should go about working for the liberation of theological education.

Second, then, let's pursue the question about what a liberative theological education means in conversation with our students. We were all once in their shoes although today's postmodern and increasingly virtual seminary classroom has decentralized the teacher and the lecture for a more connectivist, interactive, and dialogical pedagogical environment.[10] Most of us have embraced the technological revolution and implemented the opportunities such has opened up precisely because they invite, lift up, and enable faculty and students alike to be learners from one another, and this has been especially enriching as our schools have diversified.[11] But many of us are finding that while our students are attracted to the life of the mind nurtured in graduate education, they are also interested in how head knowledge transfers into heart formation and hand (ministerial or missional) activity. But herein lie both philosophic and practical sets of challenges (among others). On the one hand (here philosophically), graduate-level education has historically been focused on the achievements of the intellect, not the activism of the hands or the enthusiasm of the heart;[12] for our students to succeed, they have to discipline these latter domains or at least work hard to connect them to the former in ways that impress their judges (as faculty). Yet on the other hand (here practically), the high cost of graduate education today means either that it can be afforded only by the more affluent to begin with (i.e., those who can pay for the more leisurely activities of study and contemplation) or that alumni are saddled with having to earn middle-class incomes sufficient to repay their student debts. The point is both that seminary education is largely inaccessible to those who feel a call to ministry and that the elite who graduate are themselves funneled into a way of life that distances at least some of them from the people and contexts either from which they derived or to which some if not many of them might feel called.

Last but not least, what about the churches that seminaries serve? Here, I am referring not only to the emerging post-denominationalism at least on the North American Protestant landscape but also to the megachurch phenomenon that, like it or not, is establishing all of the standards for ministry for the present generation. While I am all for nurturing worship practices that are inclusive, dynamic, participatory, and multicultural (so that what happens in our classrooms are paralleled by what happens in our congregations and liturgies and vice versa),[13] the fact of the matter is that people are voting with their attendance and finances (tithes and offering) for forms of mega-church praise and worship experiences that are professionalized, spectatorial, and homogeneous instead. Such churches in the suburbs operate according to a middle-class modality and sensibility that is becoming normative for the seminarian afterlife (when graduates have to pay off their student loans). And in point of fact, historically, by locating seminary education at the graduate level, ministerial training was de facto defined as empowering a middle-class vocation. As preeminent historian of theological education Glenn Thomas Miller notes, graduate theological education certifies people as ministers to serve educated clientele or congregations.[14] In that respect, seminary graduates are equipped to engage with others with a similar degree or level of education, precisely the population groups of America's suburbs where cultural, racial, and ethnic differences are domesticated and accommodated into a peculiarly uniform way of life.

At this point, I am tempted to resign myself to enjoyment of my middle-class existence; I have worked hard and earned this privilege, have I not? Beyond such a self-centered response, however, the task of liberating theological education seems otherwise daunting in light of the above analysis. It would seem that all efforts to empower theological students to effectively minister the liberative power of the gospel in an unjust and pluralistic world are constrained by a variety of historical, economic, and educational factors that work subversively against our well-meaning aspirations. But to leave things here would be the reside at what M. Thomas Thangaraj calls the "disillusionment" level and not arise to the "discernment" level that I as a Pentecostal am not only committed to but have written much about.[15]

## Notes

1. I left Regent University in 2014 as a tenured professor (subject to five-year reviews) to join the faculty at Fuller Seminary, which move involves, consistent with Fuller's hiring practices, a two-year tenure review clock; given the circumstances of my transition to and welcome at Fuller, there is a sense in which I have much more job security now than anywhere or anytime before—concerns about my long-term future are the least of my worries at

present. [Note: this essay was written in early 2015, so its allusions in the text and references in the endnotes date back to events and publications from 2014 and earlier; I have not updated these for publication (in 2019) so readers ought to keep this detail in mind that the essay is appearing almost five years after it was initially written.]

2. Yong, *The Future of Evangelical Theology: Soundings from the Asian American Diaspora* (Downers Grove: IVP Academic, 2014).

3. Heltzel's two most recent books are *Jesus and Justice: Evangelicals, Race, and American Politics* (New Haven: Yale University Press, 2009), and *Resurrection City: A Theology of Improvisation* (Grand Rapids: William B. Eerdmans Publishing Company, 2012). The latter appears in Prophetic Christianity Series that Heltzel co-edits with Bruce Ellis Benson (Wheaton College) and Malinda Elizabeth Berry (Bethany Theological Seminary), which lead volume, edited by them also, was *Prophetic Evangelicals: Envisioning a Just and Peaceable Kingdom* (Grand Rapids: William B. Eerdmans Publishing Company, 2012). For the other five books in the series (so far), see the Eerdmans website: http://www.eerdmans.com/Products/CategoryCenter.aspx?CategoryId=SE!PCS.

4. See Alexia Salvatierra and Peter Heltzel, *Faith-Rooted Organizing: Mobilizing the Church for the Common Good* (Downers Grove: InterVarsity, 2013).

5. Those interested in charting the development of my thinking about Christian higher education from a Pentecostal perspective with considerations about theological education from an Asian American vantage point can compare these reflections with my previous essays, "The Holy Spirit and the Christian University: The Renewal of Evangelical Higher Education," in Gregg ten Elshoff, Thomas Crisp, and Steve L. Porter, eds., *Christian Scholarship in the Twenty-First Century: Prospects and Perils* (Grand Rapids: William B. Eerdmans Publishing Company, 2014), 163–80, and "Beyond the Evangelical-Ecumenical Divide for Theological Education in the 21st Century: A Pentecostal Assist," *Theological Education* 49:1 (2014): 87–102.

6. My use of "seminarians" in this paper is shorthand for graduate students, divinity students, and others engaged in formal theological education; similarly, "seminaries" in what follows is also inclusive of graduate programs of religion or divinity schools that educate those responding to a call to ministry.

7. In retrospect, the elitist nature of East Asian, specifically Confucian, education is unmistakable, as illumined in my essay, "Evangelical *Paideia* Overlooking the Pacific Rim: On the Opportunities and Challenges of Globalization for Christian Higher Education," *Christian Scholar's Review* 42:4 (2013): 393–409.

8. Thus does Karl Marx's castigation of the philosophic enterprise—"The philosophers have only interpreted the world, in various ways; the point is to change it" (from "Theses on Feuerbach" [1888], §XI, in W. Lough, trans., *Marx/Engels Selected Works*, vol. I [Moscow: Progress Publishers, 1969], 15, available also from https://www.marxists.org/archive/marx/works/1845/theses/theses.htm) – strike at the academic vocation as well.

9. My paraphrase of the argument in Archie Smith, Jr., "You Cannot Teach What You Do Not Know: You Cannot Lead Where You Have Not Been," in Eleazar S. Fernandez, ed., *Teaching for a Culturally Diverse and Racially Just World* (Eugene, Ore.: Cascade Books, 2014), 88–108.

10. See my essay, "Incarnation, Pentecost, and Virtual Spiritual Formation: Renewing Theological Education in Global Context," in Teresa Chai, ed., *A Theology of the Spirit in Doctrine and*

*Demonstration: Essays in Honor of Wonsuk and Julie Ma* (Baguio City: Asia Pacific Theological Seminary Press, 2014), 27–38.

11. So when Luke Timothy Johnson suggests that courses in biblical studies are now conducted, informed, and enriched by groups of students reading and exegeting scripture together from out of their various experiential and perspectival viewpoints, he alerts us to how *all* seminary classrooms, even virtual ones, are transformed when we take this principal seriously since now theological method, historiography, and ministerial and missional methods are all also similarly constituted from out of the nexus of conversations engaged by our students from their various social, historical, and contextual locations. See Luke Timothy Johnson, "Exegesis as Ecclesial Practice," in Theodore Brelsford and P. Alice Rogers, eds., *Contextualizing Theological Education* (Cleveland: The Pilgrim Press, 2008), 148–66.

12. Except perhaps in pietist circles—for example, Christopher Gehrz, ed., *The Pietist Vision of Christian Higher Education: Forming Whole and Holy Persons* (Downers Grove: IVP Academic, 2014); cf. my "Whence and Whither in Evangelical Higher Education? Dispatches from a Shifting Frontier," *Christian Scholar's Review* 42:2 (2013): 179–92, esp. 187–89.

13. For such a vision of "open worship," see Gary Rand, "Open Worship, Strategies of Hospitality and Questions of Power," in V. Esterline and Ogbu U. Kalu, eds., *Shaping Beloved Community: Multicultural Theological Education* (Louisville and London: Westminster John Knox Press, 2006), 186–98.

14. Glenn Thomas Miller, *Piety and Plurality: Theological Education Over the Last Fifty Years* (Eugene, Ore.: Cascade Books, 2014), 350–51.

15. See M. Thomas Thangaraj, "A Formula for Contextual Theology: Local + Global = Contextual," in Theodore Brelsford and P. Alice Rogers, eds., *Contextualizing Theological Education* (Cleveland: The Pilgrim Press, 2008), 98–107. My work on spiritual discernment began with my doctoral dissertation, published as *Discerning the Spirit(s): A Pentecostal-Charismatic Contribution to Christian Theology of Religions*, Journal of Pentecostal Theology Supplement Series 20 (Sheffield, UK: Sheffield Academic Press, 2000). For further reflections on theological education charting a more constructive path forward from where this essay concludes, see Yong, *Spirit-ed Theological Education: Renewing the Church from in a Networked World* (Eerdmans, forthcoming).

# CROSSCURRENTS

## BUY A FIELD
### The Future of Theological Educators

Willie James Jennings

> Then my cousin Hanamel came to me in the court of the guard, in accordance with the word of the LORD, and said to me, "Buy my field that is at Anathoth in the land of Benjamin, for the right of possession and redemption is yours; buy it for yourself." Then I knew that this was the word of the LORD.
>
> (Jeremiah 32:8 NRS)

What is the future of theological educators? This seems to me to be the urgent question pressed on us now, between the times. I prefer to focus in on the complexities that now attend being a theological educator as a way to consider the situation of theological education today. It is important to state the obvious—theological education continues unabated from the moment that humble rabbi opened his mouth and taught them, saying... We who operate in the distinction between formal and informal theological education need to remind ourselves that this is a distinction within a scholastic universe (as Pierre Bourdieu would say)[1] and, while important, it often blinds us to the vital energies of Christian and religious cultivation that are flowing through churches, mosques, temples, barber and beauty shops, music, dance, sport, and a host of other contexts and venues. We are yet in a world filled with people not only eager to talk and think about God, but also willing to press their lives (and their talent, time, and treasures) into the endeavor in belief that such talking and thinking will make a difference for them and for this world. This is a fact.

It is also a fact that formal theological education was never intended for that multitude. Even with all the historical qualifications and exceptions we might offer, it is still the case that formal theological education in the west was imagined primarily for white men and even when imagined for others it was yet in approximation of white male subjectivity.[2]

This meant the joining of two deeply incongruous visions of the desired student, one born of an undomesticated God who calls people of the multitude to lead, and another vision born of an elitism that would insure a properly ordered church and society executed through individual (masculine) genius. The suture of financial endowment and cultural assumption that held these visions together has unraveled and left us without a clear path that connects the multitude to formal theological education. There is a point of connection—theological educators. This however is precisely where we can begin to see fractures of vision but also the sites from where theological education must be rethought.

**Becoming a Theological Educator?**

The formation process of theological and religious scholars lives in the nineteenth century while we inhabit the twenty-first century. Worlds collide in doctoral study, and we have not done a good job in acknowledging and thinking about that collision. I have seen this problem through my years of being an academic dean and in my consulting work with the Wabash Center for Teaching and Learning in their Graduate Program Teaching Initiative. This collision affects everything from recruitment to job placement. It begins with the unexamined assumptions of who should be encouraged and recruited to enter doctoral study. The apprenticeship tradition that continues to inform doctoral ecologies has its strengths, but it also perpetuates myopia that severely weakens our perception of who should be a doctoral student, who doctoral students are, and who they are becoming in our programs. The selection process of doctoral students should have some element of reproduction: We will inevitably look for students whose mental architecture to some extent mirrors our own. Yet programs need to do a much better job of laying bare the assumptions of that shared mental architecture and being cognizant that we and our forms of evaluation are already embodied, already participating in antagonisms of race, class, and gender. We need forms of evaluation of potential doctoral students that reads people holistically holding together their talents, their potential to be good researcher-teachers, and their desire to connect with people. We also need forms of evaluation that challenge our myopia and that consider students whose mental frames invite us to both conceptual and pedagogical newness.

One of the most startling things I have observed in doctoral programs is the massive disconnect between who doctoral students will be as educators once they graduate (and hopefully get jobs) and who graduate faculty imagine they will be. More than one graduate faculty director told me that they are training their students to be researchers who work in tier-one research institutions when in fact the vast majority of their students work in other settings and their primary task is teaching. This disconnect means that many programs don't really think about training educators or imagining the impact of a skilled teacher as the guiding vision of their formation program. That disconnect also infects graduates who are ill-prepared to make the psychic shift from the world of their mentors to their own worlds and to embrace the teaching life as the goal of it all and not as a form of tent-making. More importantly, until doctoral programs can make the psychic shift of imagining their work of training researchers-teachers within the wider work of introducing students to the teaching life we will continue to send people into theological education already disappointed (that they have to teach) and who carry forward a tragic myopia in the way they perceive students.

**Thriving as a Theological Educator?**
Who is really paying attention to the well-being of faculty members? Almost no theological institution I know has a comprehensive plan for the development and cultivation of faculty members from the start of their career to their retirement and beyond, because almost no theological institution imagined that to be their concern. This is not to say that they are not concerned about faculty, but that concern most often translates into creating the (minimal) conditions for teaching and research —"Here is your office, there is your computer, these are the times you teach, and let me know if you need anything else." This is academic bare life, and it mimics the ideology of the American frontier where strong men and women draw on their resourcefulness and hard work to survive.

But who is thriving in the theological academy? It does not seem to be those who are relatively new to its ecology, ethnic minority women and men.

There continues to be a marked difference between the quality of life for minority faculty members and their white counterparts. Their lives in the academy mirror the demographic differences between black/brown lives on the one hand and white life on the other.[3] Few institutions have translated the awareness of the additional burdens that minority faculty members carry into concrete efforts to transform institutional ecologies. Even a cursory investigation of the physical and emotional condition of senior and mid-career minority faculty members reveals live profoundly affected by levels of stress that are grotesquely inconsistent with the leisure class trajectory of a professor. Yet this difference does not point to adjustment problems for minority faculty members but to structural problems that directly affect the witness of a theological institution and the ability of theological educators to draw on the full extent of their energy and creativity to commend theological and religious exploration to people.

The future audience for theological education will come from a deep and rich demographically diverse pool. Such a pool of potential candidates pay attention to what happens to black and brown bodies in the academy and what they often see beyond the high rhetoric of admission officers and official faculty scripts is not appealing. Schools need to start to see the care of faculty as not primarily a matter of maintenance but as fundamental to the execution of their mission. The care of the faculty is the first mission of a school.

**Connecting as a Theological Educator?**
If we need to give fresh thought to the selection and preparation of future theological educators as well as their thriving, then we do so because we have come to see them as the crucial point of connection to the multitude and the calling and wooing habits of an undomesticated God. In this regard, the division of labor has become painfully confused in theological institutions. Somewhere between expanding the number of development personnel, increasing the fundraising work of presidents and deans, and transforming faculty governance of institutions from a shared project to a burden that faculty should be relieved of, we lost

sight of a crucial skill that all faculty must cultivate together—learning how to connect with people. This is a skill not primarily of individual faculty members but of a whole faculty where colleagues help each other speak their truth to the world.

Too many schools have accepted the strange wisdom that only some in their number have the "natural ability" to speak or write or teach to a broader audience while others can communicate only to select few. Too many schools accept the church/academy distinction as a hermeneutic principle for discerning the gift and graces of colleagues and how the lines of accountability are to be drawn for them. In so doing, many schools have not only reinforced or reinscribed the same gender, race, and class hierarchies regnant in society, but also have deprived themselves of the collective wisdom and creativity of a whole faculty that may be brought to support and enhance the work of every individual faculty member. What is necessary here is more than mutual encouragement. Faculty members need to be drawn into a shared project of communication of their ideas to increasingly wider audiences with a view toward establishing an institution's unique contribution and the reason for its existence.

The point here is not the popularization of every faculty member's work, but the cultivation of an entire faculty's connecting skills. Such skills are absolutely important in our conflicted social and political situation where increasing numbers of people are being taught how not to listen. Theological educators need help and need to help each other learn how to navigate the discursive terrain of our moment in order to not only speak truth to power but also to speak to people in the everyday wonderings and wanderings of their lives. If the important work of faculty member remains relatively unknown, then that is the fault of a scholar but also of their colleagues and of a school.

I begin my thoughts with a quote from the book of Jeremiah and that strange moment in the story when the God of Israel tells Jeremiah to buy a field at an absolutely inappropriate time. The field was for a future time inconceivable at that painful moment. We need a similar gesture now. We need to turn our attention to the educators themselves and start to ask how we might allow them to be and become a wider bridge that draws together an education worth having and a God and a life of faith worth exploring.

**Notes**

1. Pierre Bourdieu and Jen-Claude Passeron, "Language and Relationship to Language in the Teaching Situation," in Academic Discourse (Stanford: Stanford University Press, 1994), 1–34.
2. I have written about these matters. Willie James Jennings, "How S hall We Teaching: The Content of Theological Education," in Eleazar S. Fernandez ed., Teaching for a Culturally Diverse and Racially Just World, (Eugene, Oregon: Cascade Books), 109–125; "The Change We Need: Race and Ethnicity in Theological Education," Theological Education, Volume 49, No. 1 (forthcoming).
3. Sara Ahmed, On Being Included: Racism and Diversity in Institutional Life (Durham: Duke University Press, 2012).

# FROM MULTICULTURALITY TO INTERCULTURALITY
## The Aim of Theological Education in Today's Global Context

vănThanh Nguyễn

"What exactly is interculturality?" It is important to acknowledge at the outset that this recently coined terminology is still very unclear for many people. First and foremost, interculturality is *not* merely "internationality" or "multiculturality" whereby a community, which is comprised of people from different nationalities or cultures, can *co-exist* side by side with each other.[1] Rather, the ideal intercultural community, which consists of members from different cultures, can *interact* with each other and thereby mutually enrich the individual members and the community as a whole.[2] Consequently, these terms—interculturality and cross-culture—are not synonymous.

I propose that theological education today must be framed by the importance of interculturality and serve interculturality within the scope of its broader aims, especially as its faculty and students become more ethnically diverse. Interestingly, the Bible contains many illustrations or stories of ideal intercultural encounter, interaction, mutuality, or exchange. Due to the limited length of this paper, I could only explore one paradigmatic example—namely Paul of Tarsus—that demonstrates genuine intercultural sensitivity and conciliatory across cultural boundaries.[3] I will then conclude by offering some pedagogical implications of teaching the Bible and doing theology in a global church and context. The overall aim of this article is to show that Paul of Tarsus is a model for teaching, living, and ministering in intercultural contexts.

**Paul a Culture Sensitive Theologian and Missionary**

Paul is surely the most influential early Christian writer and missionary. He was a diaspora Jew who was born in Tarsus (Acts 21:39), a city well known for its intellectual environment. He eventually moved to Jerusalem to be "at the feet of Gamaliel," a leading Jewish scholar of the time (Acts 22:3). Paul personally admitted that he was fully a Jew saying, "Circumcised on the eighth day, of the race of Israel, of the tribe of Benjamin, a Hebrew of Hebrew parentage, in observance of the law a Pharisee" (Phil 3:5). So much so that he persecuted the early disciples of Jesus and was determined to extinguish the Christian movement (Acts 9:1-2; Phil 3:6). But that was prior to his encounter with the risen Christ on the road from Jerusalem to Damascus.

Paul's revelatory experience dramatically changed the course of his life.[4] He was no longer the old Saul that he once was; rather, Paul was commissioned by the risen Lord to be an apostle to the Gentiles (Gal 1:12). Filled with zeal, he embarked upon various missionary journeys, which the book of Acts neatly arranged into three journeys, and founded many Christian communities or *ecclesia*. Paul also wrote many letters to these Gentile churches that he had visited in order to teach, encourage, and admonish them in their infant faith. Fourteen letters were attributed to Paul from Tarsus.[5] Through his missionary activity and writings, Paul eventually altered the landscape and transformed the religious character around the Mediterranean Basin. Gentiles gradually embraced monotheism and more importantly believed in Jesus Christ as their Lord and Savior.

No one doubts that Paul was very instrumental in the expansion of early Christianity. But the question is: "How was Paul able to influence and convince Gentile communities that had a different set of beliefs and customs to adhere to the Christian faith and way of life?" I believe that Paul was able to plant the gospel of Jesus Christ in ways that made sense and moreover intersected with the concrete aspects of the lives and cultures of his listeners. As a context theologian and missionary, he applied an "audience-sensitive approach"[6] in his evangelism. In other words, Paul contextualized the gospel within the cultural setting of his audience. This approach requires flexibility, creativity, and humility. To intellectual Greeks, he used sophisticated rhetoric for effective persuasion (1 Cor 1:17-31). To conservative and observant Jews, he appealed to the Hebrew Scriptures and applied Hebraic Midrash to explain the Torah (Gal 2:19). To those who are familiar with sports and tools of warfare, Paul used athletic (1 Cor 9:24; 2 Tm 4:7) and military (Eph 6:11-14) images and metaphors to get his message across. For ordinary folks, he used images of body parts (Rom 12:4; 1 Cor 12:12-17; Eph 4:11-16) or everyday tools (e.g., mirror in 1 Cor 13:12 and earthen vessels in 2 Cor 4:7) that everyone could understand. Although a Jew, Paul understood the paganistic world he lived in. Flemming rightfully notices that Paul was "audience-sensitive without being audience-driven,"[7] because he had the right attitude toward culture, namely, affirming as well as confronting culture. Because of these attitudes, Paul was able to be "a Jew to the Jews and as a Greek to the Greeks" (1 Cor 9:19-23). Flemming further states, "[Paul's] 'at-homeness' within overlapping Jewish, Greek and Roman environments put him in a singular position to contextualize the gospel for both Jews and Gentiles, not as a foreigner, but as a cultural insider."[8]

Paul's Areopagus speech to the Athenians (Acts 17:22-34) clearly demonstrates his cultural sensitivity and "at-homeness" with his audience and therefore serves as a compelling example of ideal cross-cultural exchange. While this comes from the book of Acts, Luke nevertheless depicts a genuine character of the historical Paul. In this missionary sermon, Paul demonstrates a willingness to interact with the worldview, belief, and practices of his audience. He began the speech by saying, "You Athenians, I see that in every respect you are very religious. For as I walked around looking carefully at your shrines, I even discovered an altar inscribed, 'To an Unknown God'" (17:22b-23). Paul is fully aware of the Athenian culture, religious beliefs, and practices. He also shows a remarkable familiarity with the Athenian's philosophical traditions by quoting well-known sayings from their philosophers and poets (see v. 28).[9] Flemming summarizes the speech in this way: "[Paul] uses this insight to respectfully engage their worldview, drawing upon indigenous language, images and concepts to communicate the gospel in culturally relevant forms."[10] While Paul takes a respectful and conciliatory approach by beginning where the audience is, Paul does not simply conform to their worldview and beliefs, but rather he seeks also to confront, correct, and transform their understanding of God. Despite Paul's painstaking effort to contextualize the gospel for his audience, the message, however, proved too much for many to accept. But it was not all a failure, for some were convinced and believed, for example "Dionysius, a member of the Court of the Areopagus, a woman named Damaris, and others with them" (v. 34).

Paul's Areopagus sermon is an outstanding example of cross-cultural evangelistic witness.[11] It also gives us a glimpse of the real Paul at his very best when it comes to cultural sensitivity and adjusting one's approach in preaching and dealing with people from other cultural backgrounds. While Paul is flexible and conciliatory in his approach, he remains firm in his interaction seeking for mutual transformation without compromising the truth of the gospel message.

### Pedagogical and Theological Implications

This article began by clarifying that real "interculturality" is more than just *co-existing* side by side with people from different nationalities or cultures. Rather, the ideal intercultural setting for interculturality provides a space or opportunity for people from different cultures to *interact* with each other and thereby mutually *enrich* and *transform* each other and those around them. With this understanding, I have explored one paradigmatic example—namely Paul of Tarsus—to illustrate an ideal biblical intercultural encounter or interaction. What follows are some pedagogical implications of teaching the Bible and doing theology interculturally in a global church and context.

As Christianity's center of gravity shifts from the global North to the global South, I suggest that we need to begin to move from a multicultural model to an intercultural model of theological education whereby people from different cultures and backgrounds do not simply co-exist but rather *interact* with each other and thereby mutually *enrich* and *transform* each other both in the classrooms and beyond. From a pedagogical viewpoint, this model requires from teachers active, sensitive, and respectful listening skills to hear the diverse voices represented in the classroom and to humbly acknowledge that such wisdom and insight can be tapped in that context.

Moreover, by applying the intercultural model of education educators recognize and affirm that there is not a single dominant perspective for doing theology or reading the Bible, but rather there are multiple or polycentric perspectives. Furthermore, by listening to the voices of all people in the church, especially to those on the periphery, for example, women and people of color, the model recognizes that everyone has something to offer to the theological endeavor and can be mutually enriched. In addition, this model not only acknowledges but also addresses the global issues of culture, class, ethnicity, and race, leading to a truly global intercultural theology.

**Notes**

1. Robert Kisala noted that "our understanding has moved from assimilation to multiculturalism to interculturality." See Kisala, "From Every Nation, People, and Language," *Verbum SVD* 53, no. 1 (2012): 37.
2. Likewise, Kisala says that "Interculturality emphasizes the mutuality of the contact between cultures, that all cultures are appreciated for the gifts they bring to humanity. It promotes the active sharing of these gifts and evaluates positively the consequent changes such sharing causes in all the cultures involved" ("From Every Nation," 37). See also his previous article entitled, "Formation for Intercultural Life and Mission," *Verbum SVD* 50 (2009): 331–35. The clarification of the term "interculturality" by Kisala is similar to other scholars' definition, for example see Hans de Wit, "Through the Eyes of Another: Objectives and Backgrounds," in *Through the Eyes of Another: Intercultural Reading of the Bible*, edited by Hans de Wit, et al. (Vrije Universiteit, Amsterdam: Institute of Mennonite Studies, 2004), 3–48.
3. For a fuller exposition, see vanThanh Nguyen, "Biblical Foundations of Interculturality," in *Interculturality*, ed. Martin Ueffing (Roscommon 25; Sankt Augustin: Steyler Missionswiissenschaftliches Institut, 2013), 37–48.
4. vanThanh Nguyen, 2010, "Evangelizing Empire: The Gospel and Mission of St. Paul," *Verbum SVD* 51, pp. 55–69.
5. Seven of the fourteen letters are undisputedly written by Paul himself: Romans, First Corinthians, Second Corinthians, Galatians, Philippians, First Thessalonians, and Philemon.
6. Dean Flemming, *Contextualization in the New Testament: Patterns for Theology and Mission* (Downers Grove, IL: InterVarsity Press, 2005), p. 92.
7. Ibid., 116.
8. Ibid., 150.
9. Scholars believe that the saying, "In him we live and move and have our being," is based on an earlier saying of Epimenides of Knossos (6th-century B.C.). As for the saying, "For we too are his offspring," it is a quote from Aratus of Soli, a third-century B.C. poet from Cilicia.
10. Flemming, *Contextualization*, 82.
11. See Lynn Allan Losie, "Paul's Speech on the Areopagus: A Model of Cross-cultural Evangelism," in *Mission in Acts: Ancient Narratives in Contemporary Context*, ed. Robert L. Gallagher and Paul Hertig, pp. 221–233 (Maryknoll, NY: Orbis Books, 2004).

# CROSSCURRENTS

## NO JOKE! RESISTING THE "CULTURE OF DISBELIEF" THAT KEEPS CLERGY WOMEN PUSHING UPHILL

Eileen R. Campbell-Reed

Early one Sunday morning in November, I stepped into the large open foyer of a progressive Baptist church in Kentucky. The staff check-in had just ended. My robe was hanging in another minister's office. I wanted a quick glance through my sermon manuscript.

Making my way across the bright room, I spotted an elderly wizened man in a dark suit. He was standing sentinel at a large table piled with blankets. I circled the table and put my hand into his gnarled one, introducing myself by name. He told me his name as we shook firmly. "Are you the Preacher Girl?" I might have sputtered a little. "Well. Hum. That sounds like a super-hero to me....? And I am definitely not a super hero! But I am your preacher today," I managed with a smile, leaning into the humor of it and keeping a grip on my ire. "I might need to see your credentials," he said slowly. Was he smiling? I could not tell. "I left them at home. I suppose you'll just have to listen to my sermon today and decide for yourself." I delivered all of this with as big a grin as I could muster. He chuckled. I had won. But it was close.

Twenty years ago, I had regular Sunday morning banter like this when I was a full-time minister in a Georgia congregation. The old men in that small-town church were like a bunch of bonus grandfathers, sharing weekly meals, running jokes, road trips, and work together on Habitat builds.

Yet, somehow it still shocks me twenty years on that such jokes linger. Surely two decades of me aging should discourage folks from calling me a girl, right? Surely being the visiting preacher for an event called "Journey for Justice" focused on women's leadership in the church, would ward off sexist jokes?

But very little has changed. Of course, banter is part of being a pastoral leader and often a fun part. But talking down to women and making jokes are also ways that white male power is maintained and propped up. It is hard to disrupt a power play—much less the culture of disbelief—when everyone is chuckling.

After five years of pastoral work, I left my small-town church to earn a PhD and become an ethnographer of ministry. As I study pastoral leadership today, I am still driven by questions like: How do women thrive in ministry when their vocations are still undermined or treated as a joke in so many parts of the church?

**Is That Still a Thing?**
"But women have come so far in twenty years, do we still have to talk about women in ministry in 2019!?" I hear this question frequently from friends who consider themselves supporters of clergywomen. They wonder aloud about other pressing and long-neglected concerns like welcoming LGBTQI+ persons into church leadership or working on racial justice.

Yet the news cycle since that Sunday I preached in Kentucky has been full of moments that capture the dual reality that women's pastoral leadership is growing, *and* women still face both jokes and more insidious backlash from working in a culture of disbelief. For example, when Rev. Heather Larson was named one of two co-pastors to succeed Willow Creek's founding pastor, Bill Hybels, the Evangelical world gawked and bristled. The usual accusations of misunderstanding the Bible, giving in to political correctness, and being unfaithful to God filled the blogosphere. A few Evangelicals like Rev. Tara Beth Leach, first female senior pastor at First Church of the Nazarene in Pasadena, California, expressed hope that Willow Creek's choice might have a more positive "ripple effect across all of evangelicalism."

In early 2018, popular Evangelical teacher, John Piper reasserted his view that women should not only avoid the pastorate, but they should also be barred from becoming seminary professors. In March, Piper blamed egalitarianism as a root cause of the fall of powerful men in the wake of the #MeToo movement. The movement is uncovering abuse and harassment in many churches and denominations, including recent accusations against Hybels, who took his retirement six months early. Predictable reactions emerged supporting and opposing Piper, Hybels, and other Evangelical leaders.

"But those are Evangelical churches," progressive Christians will say. "Women face much greater resistance to leading there." All true. And for good measure they add: "We ordain and call women! And we are not like Evangelicals!" These protests thinly veil the pervasive influence of the culture of disbelief inside progressive Christianity. In the first place, Mainline and progressive churches are a minority of America's religions (<15% of Christians), and thus, progressives are surrounded by the disbelieving culture. Women's progress inside Mainline churches is easily misinterpreted as culturally normative and misread as widespread. The root problem of sexism (not egalitarian values) remains everywhere in the religious landscape, including inside progressive churches.

When progressive Christians tell Preacher Girl jokes or protest with "Not us!" the deeper problems of sexism and social inequity for women remain unexamined. To be sure, sexism is deeply entangled with racism, homophobia, and many other injustices. No injustice can be addressed in isolation. But progressives do not have the luxury of working on racism or homophobia, as if sexism were done and over.

Evangelical and Mainline church differences aside, the number of women coming forward since 2017 to say #MeToo puts into the public eye the avalanche of harassment and abuse women face both in the church and sanctioned by the church. Just because women are ordained and hired does not mean they are fully welcomed or freed from sexism in the church.

### Women's Leadership Triples

The last major multi-denominational studies of women's church leadership appeared in 1998 and 2001. That leaves a large gap in knowledge and understanding of women's pastoral leadership in the two decades since. In 1998, Barbara Brown Zikmund, Adair T. Lummis, and Patricia Mei Yin Chang published a landmark study on women in seminary and ministry. *Clergy Women: An Uphill Calling* drew together data from predominantly white denominations and reported on attitudes about women leading the church.

In 2001, Delores Carpenter published *A Time for Honor: A Portrait of African American Clergywomen*. Carpenter's book offered the first comprehensive look at women's leadership in historic black churches. Due to challenges in procuring statistics for women's church leadership, Carpenter looked to seminary graduates to get a clearer picture of women's ministry in black churches. In her survey of seminary graduates, she found a majority of black women in the first wave of graduates went to work in predominantly white churches: United Methodist, American Baptist, and Presbyterian (USA).

In 1977, most Mainline churches were still led by men (see Fig. 1). The only denomination where women exceeded 10% of the fully credentialed clergy was the Assemblies of God. However, both Zikmund et al. and Carpenter reported impressive growth of women's pastoral leadership between 1977 and 1997.

To learn where women stood in 2017, my research assistant Sarah Reddish and I spent more than a year working through Zikmund et al.'s data to update and extend it. Like Carpenter, we also labored to find definitive statistics for black women's ordination and pastoral leadership.

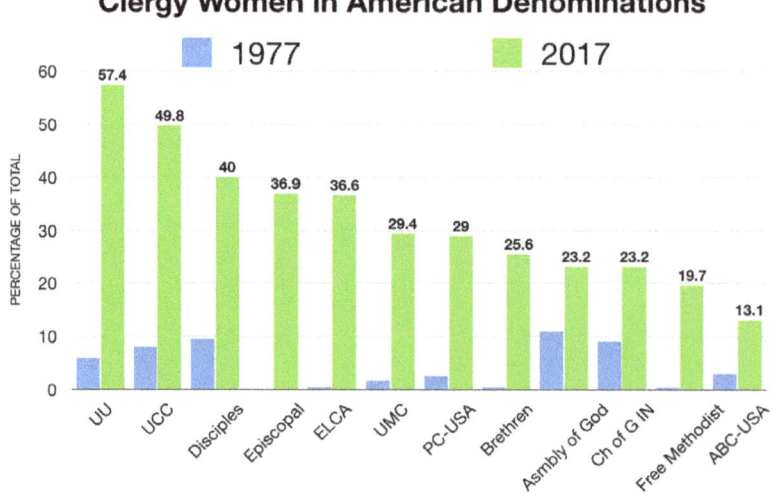

Figure 1. Growth of clergywomen in U.S. denominations (1977-2017). Source: State OfClergywomen.org. [Color figure can be viewed at wileyonlinelibrary.com]

Most of the available data about women of color come from the Association of Theological Schools (ATS) in the United States and Canada (see below).

In many predominantly white denominations, the number of clergywomen has doubled or tripled since 1997. Between 1977 and 2017, ordained women in most Mainline denominations jumped from below 10% to between 20% and 40% of the fully credentialed clergy. American Baptists are on the low end at 13%. The United Churches of Christ, as well as Unitarian Universalists, have reached a saturation point with overall numbers of clergywomen equalizing (50%) or surpassing the numbers of clergymen.

In historically black denominations, many women have to push even harder uphill as they follow God's call into ministry. For example in black Baptist churches, women are 50–75% of church members, but less than 10% of church leadership and about 1% of pastors. However, in contrast, African Methodist Episcopal (AME) churches first ordained women as elders in 1960. In 2016, they identified over 4,000 female clergy with more than 1,100 women in pastoral leadership. Since 2000, the AME has elected four women to the office of Bishop.

In most denominations, the numbers and percentages of ordained women are significantly higher than the numbers and percentages of women in the role of lead pastor (see Fig. 2). Barna's 2017 State of Pastors report estimates that about 9% of the pastors in the United States are women. In 2016, women reached a substantial enough number of total clergy (15%) for the U.S. Bureau of Labor to account for their pay in comparison with clergymen: 87 cents on the dollar, which is down from the 91 cents reported by Zikmund, et. al. in 1998.

**Seminary Enrollment and Leadership**

Parallel to the growth of women's leadership in Mainline churches, women's presence as students, faculty, and administrators in Mainline seminaries also grew dramatically starting in the early 1970s. The ATS began reporting data about gender in 1972 when women were <5 in every 100 Master of Divinity (MDiv) students and only 10% of overall seminary enrollments.

In the next twenty-five years, the numbers shot up. By 1998, thirty of every 100 MDiv students in the United States and Canada, and thirty-three out of 100 students in all seminary programs were women.

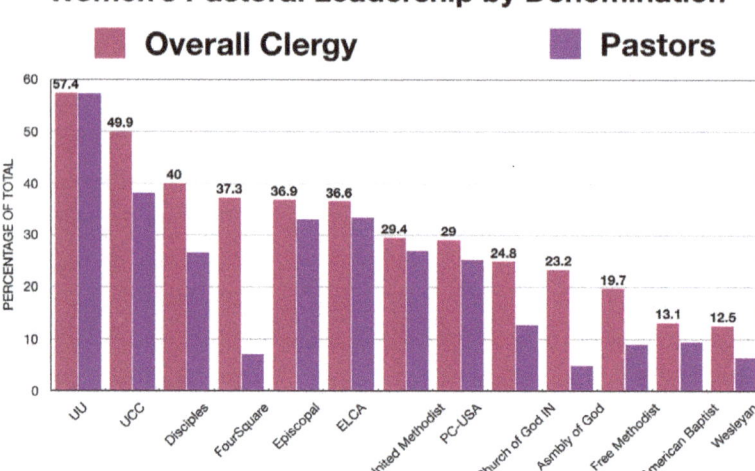

Figure 2. Comparison of women pastors and women clergy in U.S. denominations (2017). Source: StateOfClergywomen.org. [Color figure can be viewed at wileyonlinelibrary.com]

Women's enrollment in Mainline schools accelerated even more dramatically and by 1998 had approached the equalizing point with men's enrollment. From the late 1990s to the present, women in the largest Mainline seminaries have remained nearly half of the overall student population (44–49%) and half or more of the students enrolled in MDiv programs (46–52%).

Another significant change for women's enrollment in MDiv programs since the early 1970s comes into focus when we consider ethnicity. ATS reports that the numbers of Black, Asian, Hispanic, Native American, and Multi-Racial women enrolled in MDiv programs rose from less than 1% in 1973 to 7% in 1998 and to over 10% in 2016. Meanwhile between 1998 and 2017, the number of white women declined significantly: from 21% to 14% of all MDiv students. Dropping faster after the economic downturn of 2008, the number of white women enrolled in MDiv programs has declined by 40% since its peak in 2004. During the same time, numbers of white men enrolled in MDiv programs dropped by 28%.

Seminary faculty women also made dramatic gains in gender equality over the last four decades, yet growth has slowed in recent years. In 1971, women made up 12% of seminary administrators, 7% of the part-time faculty, and only 3% of the full-time faculty. In 1998, women made up nearly 20% of the full-time faculty. Yet in 2017, women are still <25% of the faculty in ATS schools.

By looking more closely at women's enrollment in Evangelical and Roman Catholic seminaries since 1998, enduring differences that reinforce a culture of disbelief are reflected in the numbers. In the ten largest Evangelical schools, women are consistently 24% of the total enrollment and 16% of the MDiv enrollment. In the ten largest Roman Catholic schools, women remain at 35% of overall enrollment, but they have dropped in the last two decades from 17% of the MDiv students to just 10%, dipping as low as 8% in 2015-16 (Fig. 3).

## Climbing Uphill in a Culture of Disbelief

In spite of women's growth in Mainline church leadership and seminary enrollment, many personal and professional hurdles continue to clutter the pathway into ministry. In particular, women face four obstacles that may sound low-impact or run-of-the-mill, yet they can be very corrosive for leadership, undermining the well-being of ministers and the people and churches they serve.

First, many churches still treat women as novelties rather than as ministers learning a spiritual and professional practice. Particularly for a new female pastor, the controversy that her hire stirs up can drain her of

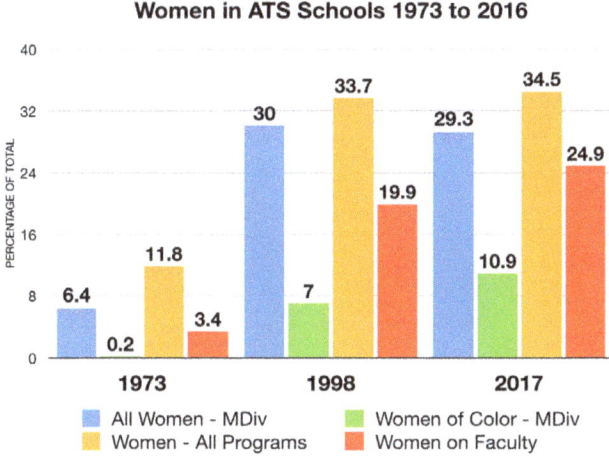

Figure 3. Growth of women's enrollment and leadership in Association of Theological Schools in the U.S. and Canada (1973-2016). Source: StateOfClergywomen.org. [Color figure can be viewed at wileyonlinelibrary.com]

energy she needs to spend getting to know her congregation and receiving meaningful feedback for on-the-job training.

A closely related problem is keeping women in isolation from supportive peers and mentors. Women are more likely to serve smaller rural and suburban churches, putting them at greater distance from other clergywomen. Yet peers and mentors are needed for perspectives that normalize ministry and advice that supports both the mundane and critical moments arising in ministry.

One of the most visible, yet unquestioned obstacles women face is the overwhelming attention to their image and how they are perceived, rather than how they embody the purpose of their work and calling. This kind of undertow comes in an endless stream of complaints about everything from the height of one's heels to the length of one's sermon to the way a pastor parents her children.

Another obstacle comes when any clergywoman, including the most accomplished and effective leaders, get dismissed because they are women. Recently, Rev. Amy Butler, pastor of Riverside Church in New York City, posted on social media, "a member of the clergy in our fine city has declined to co-officiate a funeral with me because I am a woman. The family will have two services so he can be involved." When hundreds of friends and followers expressed outrage at the overt gender bias, Butler found herself "surprised" and shocked by her own sense of the event's banality and normality.

The culture's deep-seated values of disbelief and dismissal of women are so powerful and pervasive as to creep into even the most consummate female pastors' lives. This male pastor's disdain for clergywomen may be labeled as petty, but it was a grieving family who paid the cost for his harmful actions. Together novelty, isolation, gender bias, and image perception are pillars that uphold the culture of disbelief. These and other obstacles work against women's flourishing in ministry. And they are recalcitrant to change even while they produce chronic stress in the lives of female ministers. They need to be addressed collectively for lasting change.

**Sharing the Load and Resisting the Cultural Disbelief**

Returning to my research question, we can wonder: How can women thrive in ministry vocations that are still undermined or treated as a joke in so many parts of the church? This question is not simply for individual women. It is also crucial for churches and seminaries. To reduce the load of bias women carry uphill in ministry and resist the culture of disbelief, churches and seminaries can commit to three vital steps: (1) educate everyone about implicit gender bias; (2) create supportive workspaces; and (3) focus on ministry purpose, not image perception.

First, educate everyone consistently and often about how implicit gender bias infects all areas of life including the church. We can only resist the powerful culture of disbelief in women's leadership by involving everyone intentionally in the work. Thus, helping all people in your church or seminary recognize and resist sexism in their schools, workplaces, and extended family networks will participate in uncovering and dismantling implicit gender bias.

Over the last nine years, the Learning Pastoral Imagination (LPI) Project (pastoralimagination.com) has been observing and documenting how people learn the practice ministry across time. We found one of the major roadblocks for learning ministry arises when social and personal forces of injustice undermine the minister. In particular, we have witnessed how steep the climb is for women and people of color. Not only gender bias but also deep biases based on race, class, sexual orientation, and gender identity all need education and dismantling.

In another set of research findings focused on women in business, Herminia Ibarra, Robin Ely, and Deborah Kolb, "Women Rising: The Unseen Barriers" 2014, Harvard Business Review) say: "For women, the subtle gender bias that persists in organizations and in society disrupts the learning cycle at the heart of becoming a leader." Ibarra, Ely, and Kolb also commend education for resisting implicit bias, resonating with the LPI findings.

Second, create conditions that support learning in practice, which in turn supports pastoral flourishing. In the LPI Project, we identify essential components for learning the practice of ministry, including: integration of knowledge, skill, and relational aspects of ministry; peer and senior mentoring with feedback loops about experience; and intentional space for reflection on learning.

Seminaries can re-evaluate curricular commitments by focusing on integration in classrooms, field education, and spiritual formation for everyone. Schools can attend to the implicit biases that harshly impact women, people of color, and LGBTQIA+ folks. Teaching both skills of resistance and self-caring practices will go further in preparing ministers to flourish as they lead.

Ibarra, Ely, and Kolb call the learning conditions for professional growth: "identity workspaces." They name essential workspace components for women's flourishing that include: room to examine expectations, space for experimenting without fear of failure, and a community of support.

Seminary is not the only learning space for ministers. Churches that embrace their role as a rich and vital learning environment will encourage experimentation and even failure that leads to learning. Churches can be the places where women focus on learning the practice of ministry in partnership with congregations.

Finally, to share the load and resist the culture of disbelief, churches and seminaries can help each woman anchor her ministry in a sense of leadership purpose rather than focusing on how she is perceived. Returning to the purpose for which one is called and the shared purpose of congregations to be the people of God or body of Christ is grounding to every pastor's calling in partnership with her community of faith.

For women, cultivating purpose is an antidote to over-focusing on appearances, wondering if she is "acting like pastor" or getting caught up with frustration over Preacher Girl jokes and the like. Ibarra, Ely, and Kolb point out: "Overinvestment in one's image diminishes the emotional and motivational resources available for larger purposes."

Thus, churches and seminaries in partnership with women can resist the culture of disbelief and level the pathway into ministry. Together, they can share the load of undoing implicit biases, creating supportive workspaces, and focusing on ministry purpose.

It is certainly no joke that the world needs, not superheroes, but well-prepared and well-purposed women to lead ministries of justice and care, women who believe in the love and power of God to save the world. A full report on "The State of Clergywomen in the U.S. (2018)" is available at StateOfClergywomen.org.

## CROSSCURRENTS
# THE TELOS OF THEOLOGICAL EDUCATION
## A Theological Reflection

Scott Woodward

I have been on the faculty of Oblate School of Theology for 25 years. When I began in 1990, OST offered two degrees, the Master of Divinity and the Master of Theological Studies. The school offered a few continuing education opportunities that drew small numbers from the local Church. Little thought was given to serving other than Roman Catholics. Well over 75% of the student body consisted of young men preparing for ordination in the Roman Catholic Church. Many of the 75% were Spanish-speaking men from Latin America. Some were Mexican American and others Americans of European descent. It was a rarity to see Asian or African students at that time.

The "social imaginary"[1] of the school mirrored the student population. OST viewed itself as a regional seminary primarily serving the needs of the southwestern United States. The students that came to OST largely planned to serve in parish communities with a few lay students planning to serve as hospital chaplains after achieving certification through Clinical Pastoral Education programs.[2] The unique factor at OST was that diocesan, religious, and lay students studied together, something not found in most Roman Catholic seminaries in the United States. OST also was known for preparing ministers for service within the Hispanic community, having earned a reputation for cross-cultural ministry, particularly within the Hispanic context.

Twenty-five years later, OST offers six graduate degrees, two of them doctorates. The school has a very large set of continuing education offerings attracting well over 6000 people in the past year. Drawing on previous experience in preparing students for ministry within the Hispanic community, OST now offers several specialized programs that serve particular groups. The Sophia Community program is designed to serve women who are already in ministry but lack the formative background, academic and otherwise, for ministry. The Sankofa Institute for African American Pastoral Leadership builds on the institution's cross-cultural experience, serving a population that is largely mainstream protestant. District 10 of the African Methodist Episcopal Church (AME) now sends candidates for ordination to OST, a first for both the school and the AME Church. Newly articulated programs in Hispanic theology and ministry are reinforcing earlier efforts. Doctoral students from around the world come to OST to study Spirituality in particular.

The core degree programs of the Master of Divinity and various MAs are of course still around. Roman Catholic seminarians from 12 dioceses and 4 religious communities prepare for ministry at OST, many due to the reputation for cross-cultural preparation. Today however, many of these seminarians are from Africa and Asia as well as from Latin America and the United States.[3] They study alongside Roman Catholic lay students just as those who came to OST 25 years ago did. The difference today is they also study alongside seminarians from the AME tradition, including women who are preparing for ordination. Their field education experience comes in parishes, schools, hospitals, the Bexar County jail, and a new program initiated within the Texas Department of Criminal Justice. They have theological reflection with students who are Christian but who have differing ecclesiologies, differing hermeneutics for pastoral action and scriptural interpretation, and differing church disciplines. Roman Catholic seminarians who once had little knowledge or experience with Christians from other traditions now have firsthand experience. Faculty are being challenged to include material that serves the wider Christian community, including more women, Hispanic, and African American references.

The social imaginary has changed. OST sees itself as an international center for theological study with an emphasis on mission and service to those most in need. The emphasis on mission forces an outlook that is larger than the Roman Catholic community and has challenged faculty and students alike to expand their vision. Mission involves bringing the gospel message to the world, so addressing the current issues of the world is paramount to ministerial preparation. Learning how to think theologically, pray, and interact with a global, interfaith community is now an essential ingredient within the recipe for ministerial preparation. I would argue, however, that the end is still the same as it was 25 years ago. What has changed is the context in which theological education takes place.

This is perhaps a rather long introduction to say the telos of theological education has not changed. Theological education continues to be about immersing candidates for ministry within an intense experience of the Christian way of life that moves them toward ever greater discipleship. In Roman Catholic theology, ordained ministers are expected to be models of what all are called to be as Christians, disciples of Jesus the Christ. This has not changed.

The telos of theological education then continues to be forming disciples of Jesus who carry the gospel message to the world. What has changed significantly is the context in which those disciples act and are formed. This latter change is what currently generates significant interest. The entire context of theological education is significantly different from that 25 years ago. So the issue is not that the telos has changed but rather that how the telos is achieved has changed.

Some points of explanation are due. The first point is to recall a basic principle of theological education: that it is a first-person process. Theology always involves the person him or herself in an intimate way. It involves my beliefs, my faith, and my heart and mind in ways that the study of geology, for example, does not. In short, it is an act of faith and faith is therefore affected. Since it is an act of faith, it involves conversion which leads the individual to an unknown horizon. So this intense immersion into the Christian way of life presents experiences and challenges that most students of theology do not expect. Rather than simply affirm and validate the now-present insight, it challenges that insight to move beyond and include un-imagined territory.

The challenges and questions today are, in many ways, different than they were 25 years ago. This is where the context becomes crucial. In the short description above of the difference between the student body at OST 25 years ago and today, we see some of the challenges. Today, the student body is far more international. A faculty member remarked last year that she was going to have to change her entire approach to teaching U.S. Church History since not one of her students was born in the United States. This is no longer an anomaly but rather the norm. More and more of our students are coming from the global majority in the Southern Hemisphere, Africa, and Asia.[4] These students have different experiences of Church than those from North America or Europe. Their understanding of family, marriage, and the roles of men and women in the community are different from that of the global minority. Helping students understand how these differences are lived faithfully within Christianity presents new challenges to theological education. The starting point for theological education is different.

The delivery of theological education is also very different. Students today have sources for information through the internet that provide a social imaginary, a horizon, of Christianity that may not be in accord with that of the school and/or their own tradition. If the challenges to the student's belief system, for example, become too great in theology, other sources provide salve for that soreness. The school is not the only source of information the student has for formation. This affects education in that formation has to both address the concerns of these outside sources and assist students in the interpretation of such sources. There is, however, a lot more competition for the minds and hearts of students than there was 25 years ago.

The actual context of mission and ministry reflects this change in the starting point of theological education. As noted in their text from 2005, Klimoski, O'Neil, and Schuth describe three major challenges to theological education, diversity being the first.[5] D'Antonio reports the U.S. census showed a 91% increase in the Hispanic population of the United States from 1990 to 2005.[6] Hispanics are now the largest nonwhite population group in the nation. While many self-identify as Catholic, it is safe to assume close to 100% are Christian of some variety. The theological education process for Christians must take this new context into account. The context of ministry in terms of language, culture, and customs must be addressed in ways that reflect the changing population graduates will serve.

Klimoski describes four elements of diversity that affect theological education as reported by educators themselves: heritage, culture, education, and church experience.[7] Heritage includes family, ethnic, and religious background as well as age and personality. Culture involves place of origin as well as socioeconomic class, language, intercultural experience, and attitude toward culture. Education describes not only educational background but also learning experiences, learning style preferences, and openness to learning. Church experience holds the worship preferences and experiences, theological position, spiritual experiences, and ministerial images[8] students bring to theological education. Each of these "diversities" holds considerable sway over how we approach teaching and learning with each student. I frequently hear faculty saying a certain student's "experience of Church" is too small. By that they usually mean it is limited by his or her culture or spirituality in ways that do not address the reality of the Church the student will serve. A graduate of theological education must be prepared to address cross-cultural demands in ways not known before. Whether it be a pastor from Nigeria who leads an Hispanic-majority church, an Anglo pastor who leads an African American-majority church, or a pastor from India serving in an Anglo-majority church, cross-cultural ministry is here and part of the current demand on theological education.

The indicators Klimoski lists and the locus of ministry described by D'Antonio present a new context for discipleship. They are but a few of the issues facing theological education. A growing group of institutionally disaffected persons are making the "spiritual but not religious" category one that demands attention. The "nones," that is, those who profess no religious affiliation, are growing in number as well.[9] In 1990, San Antonio had one mosque. Today, it has nine along with a Sikh temple, three Buddhist temples, and two Hindu temples. It is far more likely today than it was in 1990 that those our graduates serve will address someone from one of these other religious traditions. Theological education has to help students have a way of navigating such an experience without losing touch with their own tradition. That, too, is a form of cross-cultural preparation.

What has been presented here is more of a theological reflection on the telos of theological education than anything else. It does not pretend to offer a new end. Rather, it portends to describe the new context of living as a disciple of Jesus. The message of Christ is eternal. How it is lived is defined by each successive generation through the lens of their experience. That is what I believe is happening with theological education today. It continues to have the eternal task of building disciples who live as examples of what all are called to be, but it takes place within an ever-changing context.

**Notes**

1. Charles Taylor uses the term "Social Imaginary" to describe the collective image that provides for a self-understanding. See Charles Taylor. The Secular Age. (Harvard University Press: Cambridge, MA, 2007), 146.
2. In Fall 1990, OST had a headcount of 95 students in the Master of Divinity and Master of Theological Studies. Of these, 34 were of Hispanic descent, 56 were of European descent, 6 were of Asian descent, and one was of African descent. Twenty-eight were women. International students are not noted in these statistics. Statistics from Unpublished Material, OST Student List, Fall 1990.
3. In Fall 2014, OST had 62 seminarians from four religious communities and 12 dioceses in the United States. Of the 62 seminarians, 31 are non-U.S. residents from 11 different countries. Thirty-three are Hispanic from the United States and Latin America, 10 are Asian, 1 is African American, 8 are African, and 10 are White. From Unpublished Material. OST Student List, Fall 2014.
4. Bishop Ricardo Ramirez, CSB, and Kathy Brown both address these changes in their reflections on conclusions from the Keystone Conferences. See Victor J. Klimoski, Kevin J. O'Neil, and Katarina M. Schuth. *Educating Leaders for Ministry: Issues and Responses*. (Liturgical Press: Collegeville, MN, 2005), 177–184.
5. Klimoski, xi–xii.
6. William V. D'Antonio et al. *American Catholics Today: New Realities of Their Faith and Their Church*. (Rowman and Littlefield Publishers: Lanham, MD, 2007), 165.
7. Klimoski, 11–25.
8. I would call this the social imaginary they have of ministry.
9. Cary Funk and Greg Smith. "'Nones' on the Rise: One in Five Adults have no Religious Affiliation", Pew Research Center's Forum on Religion and Public Life. (Pew Research Center: Washington, DC, October 9, 2012), accessed December 28, 2014, http://www.pewforum.org/2012/10/09/nones-on-the-rise/

CROSSCURRENTS
# TEACHING OTHER FAITHS ABOUT ISLAM
A Transformative Journey

Zainab Alwani

Over the course of the last century, we have witnessed a revival of religion and religious traditions, contrary to speculations about the gradual decline of religion in society. While in the fifties, the religious landscape of America was reflected in Will Herberg's book, Protestant, Catholic, and Jew, in the sixties, theologians were talking about the impact of secularization on religion and theology. The dominant theories expected religion to decline, especially in the public realm, and thought that it should be marginalized, limited to private life, and the development of religion would be succeeded by science. Today, in American academia and the public sphere, we are witnessing the study of world religions, interreligious dialogues, comparative religion studies become part of the educational curriculum.[1]

Religious education remains a core component of society's advancement toward cultural competency when education requires us to look beyond our own faith traditions and into the interfaith domain. Although many faiths have a fundamental aspect of proselytizing to spread their truth to others, religious education in interfaith settings is often regarded as the indispensable work of a pluralistic society. There are extensive academic traditions of biblical literacy to narrate the stories and passages of the Bible, just as there are scholarly endeavors to learn the Hebrew Scriptures and recognize the early conceptualizations of faith and justice as recognized by Jews. These are earnest attempts to know others by knowing their faith traditions. It is through this legacy that I draw on my own motivations to teach the Qur'ān to interfaith audiences of Christians,

Jews, and others in the Howard University School of Divinity. In today's context of religious illiteracy compounded with anti-Muslim sentiment, my work reflects a larger implication toward religious equity and justice in a pluralistic society.

Howard University School of Divinity (HUSD) is one of the oldest fully accredited (1940) theological schools affiliated with the Association of Theological Schools in the United States and Canada. As one of the 13 schools and colleges within Howard, it is the only African American theological school connected to a comprehensive category one research institution. Although Howard University is widely reflective of the growing significance of Islam in the United States and within its student, staff, and faculty composition, it was not until 2011, when the Howard University School of Divinity (HUSD) established a Master of Arts (M.A.) in Islamic studies and hired, for the first time in its history, a Muslim professor to lead the new initiative. It became the first of its kind among the Historically Black Theological Institutions (HBTI).

As the first Muslim scholar and the founding director of the Islamic Studies at Howard University, I understand the challenges are great and my responsibility is vast because my role is critical to the growth and trajectory of the entire program. Since I joined the HUSD community in 2011, my goal has been to implement the vision of the school to the best of my ability. This has placed students and faculty at the forefront of current events and intriguing conversations within the Christian, Muslim, and other faith communities. The program's extensive course work and authentic, hands-on methodologies continue to foster critical thinking. The HUSD faculty has recently voted to include Islamic Studies courses among those required for the M.Div. and M.A. degree programs.

As I believe that humanity is one family, it is my goal to build bridges between the different religious, social, and cultural perspectives through genuine interaction and *ta'āruf* (the Qur'ānic concept of getting to know each other). This has manifested itself in my teaching, scholarship, and helping my students prepare for lives of faithful witness and public service. The purpose of this paper is to discuss how I teach Islam in a rich pluralistic environment, what I teach and how I evaluate my teaching.

## Contemporary critical questions: humanity seeking answers

The main challenge that confronts scholars is how to understand the sacred texts. A follower of faith should internalize this worldview and virtues in order to become a loving, just and disciplined citizen of the society. As a faith community, how do we evaluate our performance in our world today? How do we read and interpret our sacred scriptures? How do we as religious scholars read the sacred texts of other faiths without violating their integrity? As a Muslim scholar, what do I teach my students from different faith communities about the Qur'ān? How, and in what manner should this book of scripture be approached and in what ways could it impart significant purpose and meaning for readers of different faith traditions? How could a better understanding of this sacred text contribute toward a more dignified life for others, to less conflict and wars and to greater success of peace efforts today? How do we come together to build a worldview on a moral, ethical, and peaceful world? How do we define morality and ethics in a world full of confusion?

In exploring such questions, I advance the following propositions: (1) Rather than attempt to develop narratives that may divide humanity, religious leadership should devote energies to strengthening unity through developing theology of tolerance, creating team-taught courses, and continuing conversations on crucial global issues that impact humanity at large within a framework of mutual caring; and (2) activists, religious and civil leaders, must work together to ensure that support services can meet pressing demands without downgrading the interests of any group.

In my courses on the Qur'ān, we seek to understand its overall paradigm that communicates ethics, morality, theology, religious decrees, and a faith-based social order. Unlike any other book, the Qur'ān demands its reader to both seek to understand and seek to transform. There are numerous passages/*ayat* that communicate the complexity of the religion of Islam. The Qur'ān also outlines the essential components of a faith-based social order, organizing family structures, marriage relationships, community leadership, and social laws and regulations. For English-speaking audiences, there is a heavy reliance on translations to interpret the original message of the Qur'ān, which was revealed in classical Arabic that predates Islam. Given that translations vary in form and content, and depend on human interpreters, it is critical to understand which translations should be used in which instances. Sometimes it could take a combination of multiple translations to get a clear picture of the true meaning and intent behind what is being said in Arabic. This exercise requires a professional who is trained in Quranic Arabic, which I have taught many times over the years. Therefore, I read with the students from different translations; the more successful translated versions they read, the closer they get to the original text. It also trains them to double- and triple-check a translation that does not coincide with the overall theme and harmony of the chapter. My instructional focus in interfaith classes is to teach students how to identify the core elements of Islam through active engagement with the Qur'ān. I strive to communicate that the Qur'ān is accessible to all of its readers when it is read with the intention of both understanding and transformation.

The Qur'anic message clearly defines the three important relationships between God, humanity, and the universe and then regulates these in such a way that develops an integrated *tawḥīdī*-based society. The Qur'ānic narrative of the relationship with God started with the Covenant to believe in Him alone (Q; 7:172). The essence of this relationship is rooted in monotheism/*tawḥīd* believing and affirming God's oneness and existence. Here, God wants us to worship him by our own free will trust *(Amaanah)*; "We did indeed offered the Trust to the heavens, the earth and the mountains, but they refused to bear it, and were afraid of it. Yet human accepted it; (33:72). Once humanity accepted the responsibility, God entrusted us as His trustee/stewards on earth"; "Remember When your Lord said to the angels, I am putting a trustee *(Khalifah)* on earth," (2:30). The Qur'ān explains to us our nature: Consider the human self, and how it is formed in accordance with what it is meant to be, (7) and how it is imbued with moral failings as well as with consciousness of God! (8) To a happy state shall indeed attain he who causes this [self] to grow in purity, (9) and truly lost is he who buries it [in darkness] (91:7-10).

The Qur'ān tells us that the angels were concerned that humanity may corrupt the beautiful world and spill blood. God, with His ultimate knowledge and wisdom, assured the angels that He knows what they don't know. He emphasized His trust in humanity (2:30). People were equipped to determine what's right or wrong; however, they sometimes read it in light of their desire, pain, or pleasure and it may lead to wrong conclusions. The Qur'ān teaches that God has given people the freedom to choose which path to take in every decision of life. He has also outlined the consequences of these choices. God has ordained accountability for humans on the Day of Judgment, He will judge us according to the choices we make in this life, not the decisions of others. The Quran confirms this as: "Whoever does righteousness – it is for his [own] soul; and whoever does evil [does so] against it. And your Lord is not ever unjust to [His] servants." *(41:46)*. As a result, each human being, whether male or female, is directly accountable to God for his or her behavior. The foremost quality of mind and character that flows from this commitment is a state of constant vigilance or an awareness of the presence of God, the All-Knowing. A holistic reading of the Islamic text shows that all previous messages brought to humanity by their respective prophets and messengers call for these same values (i.e., *tawḥīd*/monotheism, *Tazkiah*/purification, and *Umran*/cultivation of earth and protect the creations of God). Therefore, humanity's duties and obligations and performance will be evaluated according to these higher values. It is important to emphasize that people are equipped to interact with the universe in a way that actualizes *stewardship* duties and establishes the feelings of closeness and harmony between humanity and universe.

The Qur'ān clearly explains that humankind's mission on earth is to establish an effective stewardship, while acknowledging that all men and women are created equal in worth and value regardless of race, gender, or class, and affirming that one's *taqwā* (piety) is the only feature that determines one's superiority over another person (whether man or woman). Religion provides guidelines, an external, stable source that is beyond human's desires. Though religion has no monopoly on morality, it does condition our common environment and shape our notions of right and wrong. Religion promotes the social virtues like truth, honesty, justice, equality, piety, service, love, discipline, etc.

In this complex and confusing time, we as academics, people of faith and teachers have a great responsibility toward humanity and nature. The Quran says: "O you who have believed, Be ever steadfast in your devotion to God, bearing witness to the truth in all equity; and never let hatred of any-one lead you into the sin of deviating from justice. Be just: this is closest to being God-conscious. And remain conscious of God: verily, God is aware of all that you do. (5:8).

We have been entrusted to look out for each other, as residents under a sky-painted roof. In the Prophetic tradition, Prophet Muhammad explains the responsibility of saving the ship: "The parable of those who respect the limits of Allah and those who violate them is that of people who board a ship after casting lots, some of them residing in its upper deck and others in its lower deck. When those in the lower deck want water, they pass by the upper deck and say: If we tear a hole in the bottom of the ship, we will not harm those above us. If those in the upper deck let them do what they want, then they will all be destroyed together. If the people do not stop them, they will all fall and be failures, but if they stop them they will all be saved."

**The particularity of teaching the Qur'ān in a western context**
Teaching the Qur'ān to interfaith audiences is distinct from other interfaith religious education experiences because there are considerations that are solely associated with teaching a marginalized faith that is simultaneously targeted and misunderstood. Even though Islam is the second most practiced religion on earth, it can easily be described as the most misunderstood. Stereotypes, prejudices, and false associations continue to target Muslims and their faith in Islam. My work to teach the Qur'ān becomes an effort to correct the wrong assumptions deeply rooted in misunderstandings while at the same time introducing the truth of the Qur'ān.

Anti-Muslim sentiment is pervasive in our current context and it causes interfaith students to question the integrity of the Qur'ān and its essence of goodness. With media outlets and government leaders suggesting that Islam is a religion of violence and anti-Western values, people in larger society begin to assume that all aspects of the faith must be harmful— particularly targeting the Qur'ān. Teaching this unique text becomes not just an effort of religious education, but an advancement of religious social justice to frame Islam, Muslims, and the Qur'ān as manifestations of the goodness of God Almighty.

The Qur'ān describes itself as a message to all of humanity, even if society suggests that it is the book for Muslims. In religious education spaces, students come to study the Qur'ān assuming that it will only help them better understand Muslims and Islam. I use my classroom to demonstrate that the verses of the Qur'ān contain lessons to transform all of humanity because it is the completion of the final message of The One, God Almighty.

Islam is the culmination of the Abrahamic faith traditions, following Judaism and Christianity. When teaching the Qur'ān, I am able to center its messages in conversation with the Old Testament and the New Testament to show continuity and distinctions. Fostering a Qur'ānic dialogue across faiths inspires relevant and transformative interfaith relationships that ground a pluralistic society in faith, truth, and justice.

Teaching the Qur'ān has never simply meant translating a text nor delineating Islamic faith requirements. Teaching the Qur'ān in today's interfaith context advances religious equity by denouncing stereotypes, addressing misunderstandings, and positioning Islam in the body of faiths that communicate the Oneness of God and the Unity of His Message.

## *What I teach*

My teaching philosophy welcomes the ensuing debates, disagreements, and exchanges of ideas because I believe this is the best way to understand one another and truly grow together as a community. In this context, I argue that there are pressing needs to ensure that our students understand the other faiths from their own sources.

I begin all my courses by building the foundation, teaching my students the Qur'ānic worldview, its message and values. The Qur'ānic worldview explains the relationship between God the Creator of the heavens and the earth, humankind and the universe. Humanity is viewed in the Qur'ān as one family existing in a state of kinship. Men and women are equal in their origin and identity, and in their duties in the purpose of creation. All people are created equal in worth and value regardless of race, ethnicity, gender, or class. This allows the students to examine and evaluate all the Muslim practices, interpretations, cultures, laws, and lifestyles in light of the Qur'ān. Human beings are equipped to interact with the universe in a way to establish feelings of harmony between humanity and the universe. God made it possible for human beings to expand their energies to make sense of the physical world, utilizing its power for the common good, uncovering its laws, and developing methodologies for dealing with revelation. This method has proven to be successful throughout my teaching career.

Muslims regard the Qur'an as the last divine speech revealed by God and it was not revealed to any specific group of people, culture, or religion. It came with a message that is universal to an audience that comprises of all humanity. By addressing Christians and Jews as "People of the Book," the Qur'an recognizes that there are other religious communities that have previously received divine guidance. The students learn that Islam is a continuation of the message received by previous prophets, stretching back from Abraham, Noah, Moses, and Jesus, peace be upon them all. The prophetic mission takes as its starting point the belief in the oneness of God "Tawhid." The Qur'an presents Muhammad as a prophet sharing a lineage of previous prophets sent to humankind. The purpose of these prophetic narratives is to underscore the unity of the mission of prophethood, the unity of their message, and the unity of their Divine source.

The Qur'an does not shy away from dialoging and presenting its arguments supported by evidence and requesting the same from its opponents. Therefore, I train my students to read the Qur'an and have an honest dialogue with it, and pose all their questions and concerns freely. Because my students are new to the study of Islam, concept maps make explicit integration of old and new knowledge. I foster critical thinking, facilitate the acquisition of lifelong learning skills, and prepare students to function effectively in any situation to help them develop their problem-solving skills. I utilize concept maps as one of my teaching methods to aid students in generating ideas, designing complex structures, and communicating complex ideas. I have found it to be a very effective method in the area of comparative religions.

## How I teach

I try to match my teaching style with that of the Qur'ān, leveraging various methods to teach my students about Islam and the Qur'ānic worldview. I have found *questioning activities* to be particularly helpful because this method encourages students to learn how to formulate the right questions and look for the answers in the Qur'ān. There are no limitations on what or how many questions to ask, and no judgments or criticism of questions. This method helps increase student productivity and motivation. As students focus on what they want to discover, they learn how to generate more pointed questions and that help get them their answers without prodding. Questions can be general or based on a particular topic or reading exercise. The questioning activities are used while responding to reading assignments or analyzing documentaries. This teaching method has proven to be very effective.

Interfaith dialogue is also central to my teaching methods. I would argue that this method is used by the Qur'ān itself.. In 2011, the Interfaith *World Café Dialogue* model was introduced to the HUSD community for the first time. I employed the World Café Dialogue model and organized a series of interreligious dialogue events. These events served three objectives: (1) to dispel the myths and misunderstandings among our communities; (2) to promote mutual respect and understanding; and (3) to build trust between our communities in order to work together on solving complex social problems. One of the programs we organized draws together notable Christian and Muslim scholars, interreligious community professionals, along with Howard University and Washington Theological Consortium students in an engagement of small group dialogue that expanded one's world view, while renouncing fear and distrust. I invited an interfaith leader Taalibah Hassan, to facilitate and help train the students in this new field. All the students were involved in this activity and worked enthusiastically. Since most of my students were community leaders, it was an effective channel to teach and train them. The students' evaluation of the event was great and the students provided valuable comments and suggestions for the future events. The World Café' Dialogue is one of many innovative activities, field trips, or lectures I coordinated as part of the Islamic studies courses at the School of Divinity. While we offer customary coursework in Qur'ānic studies, Ethics, Women Studies, Hermeneutics, Islamic Jurisprudence, and the Arabic language as requirements, additional trending classes in Chaplaincy and other interreligious courses attract both Christian and Muslim students are in the works.

Interfaith dialogue was a big part of my own personal journey. My first interfaith encounter was in Baghdad, Iraq, when I was a little girl. We used to live in a pluralistic neighborhood mostly populated by Christians. My father was an Imam who was known for his strong stances against injustice, where he would speak on behalf of the voiceless and this caused his popularity grow among the minorities in the area. Our Christian neighbors would listen to his Friday Sermons and come over afterward to discuss/question what he had talked about. I was always amazed at the mutual love and respect they had for each other. We moved to Egypt when I was in 7th grade. The principal of the school I attended was a Coptic Christian, who became one of my role models. He always showed the utmost respect to learning and understanding to the Islamic faith. He encouraged me to recite verses of the Qur'ān in the morning, and to my surprise, he would correct me if I made any mistakes in my recitation. He would refer to the Qur'ānic principles and values in his disciplinary speeches and other occasions. My childhood experiences with interfaith dialogue really opened my eyes to the amount of knowledge and admiration that could be gained from wanting to understand each other's faiths. This mentality opened the doors of love and respect for my fellow humans of faith, and I invite my students to have similar experience that will positively affect their lives and their relationships with one another.

Another method I like to use is *co-teaching*. I have co-taught three courses thus far. The first course was on "Prophethood in the Bible and in the Qur'an" with Dr. Cain Hope Felder, which was unique in its nature and structure. It was a wonderful academic and theological experience. The African American theological debate on the subject was incredible. This course should be considered as the cornerstone of the field of theology, world religion, philosophy, and interreligious studies. The second course was with Dr. Alice Bellis "Women in the Hebrew Bible and the Qur'an." Reading and discussing both the Hebrew Bible and the female perspective on the Biblical stories enriched both the instructors and the students. The theological debate among feminists, womanists, and general theologians in the Hebrew Bible and the Qur'ān was incredible. This course is also considered the cornerstone of the field of interreligious studies and dialogue. Two years ago, I designed a new course called "Sacred Text and Hermeneutics" along with two distinguished colleagues. "Sacred Text and Hermeneutics" was a team-taught course with Professor Gay Byron and Professor Cain Hope Felder (prior to his retirement). Since I joined the HUSD and discovered the wealth of knowledge among the faculty, I have been trying to find a way to share it with our students. It was the first team-taught course about Sacred Texts and Hermeneutics offered at the School of Divinity, which was led by three professors in Biblical and Qur'ānic Studies. The course examined hermeneutical theories, exegetical methods, and theological perspectives from different HUSD professors. Each class session included a lecture on a particular sacred text and its methods, as well as an interactive opportunity for students to engage the professors and each other on the hermeneutical insights and other implications of the material. This course is considered to be the cornerstone of the field of theology, hermeneutics and interreligious studies and dialogue. It's been an honor to help move the needle forward with respect to religious and interreligious studies.

Indeed, my first experience in teaching team-taught course was back in 2006 at the Washington National Cathedral. I was invited by Rev. Michael Wyatt to teach for the first time in the history of the Cathedral about The Five Pillars of Islam. It was a comparative religion course. It was beautifully described: "In Islam, the Five Pillars of Religion are guidelines for living in accordance with God's will. In Christianity, these principles also exist but in quite different form and emphasis. In this course, find yourself journeying side by side as Christian and Muslim compare the practices of a devout life." I also include in my teaching, activities such as site visitation, students' presentations, and interviews. I also invite guest speakers and encourage the students to attend conferences and seminars, educational games, and other methods to engage the students. In my courses, I share my research with students and guide the students on their original research.

## How I evaluate my teaching

I evaluate my teaching through the students' growth intellectually, spiritually and socially.

One time, Karen, one of my students said to me: "Dr. Alwani your class made me a better Christian and a better person. I increased my prayers especially when I had a problem with my son and his girlfriend whom I disapproved of. She had no place to go and my son was begging me to let her live with us in my big house. I have been refusing until last week when you started discussing the meaning and the role of family and the (*ummah*) community in protecting every member of it. My heart has changed and decided to welcome her in my home. I felt at peace and regained peace with my son. I felt I saved a life, what a beautiful feeling!"

Elizabeth, another student of mine who takes her work seriously told me after a few sessions, "Dr. Alwani, I have a dream that you and me take a year off and travel to teach people that we are one, carrying the message of God, to make this world a better place for everyone and everything."

My student James wrote a post about his experience at: http://jamesthomassnyder.com/tag/zainab-alwani/

My student Ardaine came to class with his own biases and argued about everything. I encouraged him to challenge me and ask any questions or state any objections he had. He also agreed to be challenged. At the end, he decided to leave all the obstacles that blinded his view and he wrote a wonderful paper about marriage and family in Islam. This made him a believer not with blind faith, but with a critical mind and high spirit.

Rev. Lee, one of my first students at Howard, used to take notes and teach his congregation what he learned about morality, building characteristics and strong families and communities. My student Michael who expressed his appreciation of the structure of family and the *(ummah)* community (Ummah) in Islam as he stated in his remarks at the HUSD Faculty Student Colloquium Spring, 2014. http://divinity.howard.edu/pdf_forms/2014_Spring_Divinity_Magazine.pdf.

These are a few examples of the product of an honest and true interreligious dialogue. More than 60 percent of my students take more than one of my courses. I believe that is the best indicator of success and I know every one of my students will make our world a better place.

**Conclusion**

By their very nature, people are inquisitive. The goal of education should be to encourage seeking answers, as it is in this way that we advance. I facilitate this advancement of knowledge. I believe that the role of religious scholars is to guide by example. Teachers impart more by way of example than content, and students are very perceptive in recognizing when a teacher does not practice what she preaches. Unless there is a climate of mutual respect in the classroom, students will be very reluctant to add to the conversation. Therefore, as theologians, we need to create a learning environment in which students feel safe, yet engaged. This means they are free to contribute to the class and develop their ideas. In this context, we may come together to build a worldview on a moral, just and peaceful world.

## Useful references

For more information on best practices in teaching interfaith courses, see: http://www.bu.edu/rct/files/2012/08/2012-Consultation-Executive-Summary.pdf Boston University School of Theology **2012 Consultation Executive Summary**

"The Formation of Interfaith Just Peacemakers: A Working Consultation"

http://www.ats.edu/uploads/resources/publications-presentations/chapp-reports/boston-university.pdf

## Notes

1. The religious diversity became part of the American culture and the academic institutions responded to that diversity in promoting pluralism's initiatives and projects. Since 1991, Diana Eck has been heading a research team at Harvard University to explore the new religious diversity of the United States and its meaning for the American pluralist experiment. The Pluralism Project has been documenting the growing presence of the Muslim, Buddhist, Hindu, Pagan, Sikh, Jain, and Zoroastrian communities in the United States.
2. http://divinity.howard.edu/about_us.html.
3. " O humankind! Be conscious of your Sustainer, who has created you out of one living entity, and out of it created its mate, and out of the two spread abroad a multitude of men and women. And remain conscious of God, in whose name you demand [your rights] from one another, and of these ties of kinship. Verily, God is ever watchful over you! Q 4:1".
4. "O humankind! Behold, We have created you all out of a male and a female, and have made you into nations and tribes, so that you might come to know one another. Verily, the noblest of you in the sight of God is the one who is most deeply conscious of Him. Behold, God is all-knowing, all-aware. Q 49:13".
5. "O humankind! Worship your Sustainer, who has created you and those who lived before you, so that you might remain conscious of Him (21) who has made the earth a resting place for you and the sky a canopy, and has sent down water from the sky and thereby brought forth fruits for your sustenance: do not, then, claim that there is any power that could rival God, when you know [that He is One] Q 2:21 -22" .
6. "When your Lord brought forth offspring from the loins of the Children of Adam and made them bear witness about themselves, He said, "Am I not your Lord?" They replied, "We bear witness that You are." This He did, lest you should say on the Day of Resurrection, "We had no knowledge of that" Q 7:172".
7. Qur'ān:18:29-31.
8. Qur'ān 49:13, 87:14, 35:18.
9. Z. Alwani, *Maqāṣid Qur'āniyya*: A Methodology on Evaluating Modern Challenges and Fiqh al-Aqalliyyāt, in *The Muslim World*, vol. 104 (Hartford Seminary: October 2014 ), 465-487 https://onlinelibrary.wiley.com/doi/full/10.1111/muwo.12073.
10. "But seek, with the (wealth) which God has bestowed on you, the Home of the Hereafter, nor forget your portion in this world: but do the good, as God has been good to you,

and seek not (occasions for) mischief in the land: for God loves not those who do mischief."
Q 45:13, 28:77.

11. Source: Ṣaḥīḥ al-Bukhārī 2361.

12. THE FIVE PILLARS OF ISLAM: *A course with Zainab Alwani, Michael Wyatt and others Mondays, 18 Sept. - 16 Oct., 7-9 pm, Perry Auditorium,* http://www.cathedral.org/pdfs/HE060820.pdf.

## CROSSCURRENTS

# "KNOWING WHO," A SERMON ON PROVERBS 8:1-21

Ted A. Smith

This sermon was preached in Cannon Chapel at the Candler School of Theology at the first worship service of a new school year.

By now you've surely seen the syllabi. As a student, you know what's coming. If you are a faculty member, you know your enrollments and your committee assignments. And if you are a staff member, you know what you have to get done this semester. This week. Today. For all of us, the due dates are already bearing down. You may have wondered if you had time to come to chapel today. I did.

But we are here—in this school, in this room, at worship—because Wisdom calls us. We have heard Wisdom call, and we long to answer her.

Proverbs 8 gives voice to one of the deepest convictions Christians have: that God wants to be known. God does not hide from Adam and Eve; they hide from God. God wants to be known. God delivers the children of Israel from slavery and gives them a law that makes clear God's hopes for the world. For God wants to be known. When we break that law, God sends prophets to help us see what God is doing in the world. For God wants to be known. And in the fullness of time, God comes among us as one of us, Jesus of Nazareth, Word made flesh. For God wants to be known.

Proverbs 8 is part of this great string of stories. Wisdom wants to be known. She is not hidden away, surrounded by traps, like some kind of secret treasure that might or might not be found by a few lucky, plucky souls. No! Wisdom stands in broad daylight in the middle of our busyness. She calls out from the heights, the gates, the crossroads (vv. 2-3).

Her cry is to all that live (v. 4). She loves those who love her (v. 17). Wisdom wants to be known. The God who comes to us in Jesus Christ wants to be known.

That makes knowing God different from other kinds of knowledge. For a fact does not hope that we discover it. A method, no matter how excellent, does not seek us out. Data does not love us back. But God ... God wants to be known. Wisdom calls us. Wisdom loves those who love her. And so seeking Wisdom is different from other kinds of learning.

Let me try a shabby typology of the kind to which professors are prone, a typology that won't hold the weight of reality but still might fail in interesting ways. Within that kind of typology, let me say that most of our knowing can be grouped into one of three different modes of knowing: knowing that, knowing how, and knowing why. For the Kantians in the house, I mean something like pure reason, practical reason, and judgment. For the Platonists: the true, the good, and the beautiful. For the rest of us: knowing that, knowing how, and knowing why.

These modes of knowing start early in our culture. Kids in grade school learn *that* 8+7=15. They learn *how* to do things like "regroup" when adding 3-digit numbers. And they look at these funny pictures of blocks grouped in hundreds, tens, and ones that are supposed to teach them *why* all this works. They learn facts, techniques, and reasons to do things this particular way. If it all works, they know that, how, and why.

These modes continue to shape our knowing as we move through life. Maybe—and this fate has befallen some of my best friends—maybe you end up in law school, for instance. Law students might learn that *Terry v Ohio* held that police had to have "specific and articulable facts"—not just a hunch—to justify stopping and frisking someone. They might learn how to write a brief defending someone who has been illegally stopped and frisked. And they might, in a jurisprudence class, learn some reasons why this standard contributes to a good society. Good law students come to know that, how, and why. From pre-K to graduate and professional schools of many kinds, knowing that, knowing how, and knowing why order the ways we come to know our world.

But in Proverbs 8 Wisdom sings of knowing in a different register. Wisdom promises knowing that, how, and why. Come to me, she says, and I'll teach you all three. But Wisdom offers something more: you will know me, she says. You will know me. And, she says, I love those who love me. Learning Wisdom means knowing that, knowing how, knowing why ... but even more, it means knowing who. Not just knowing who wrote Genesis or Ephesians or whatever else ... but knowing who is the life and order at the heart of all things. Wisdom does not just call us to know *about* her. She calls us to know *her*. Herself. For God wants to be known.

Knowing who is different from other kinds of knowledge. It is not just another bead that can be added to the string that already holds knowing that, how and why. It is more like the string itself. Wisdom, in the sense that Proverbs describes and in the sense that we seek, is of a different order.

Wisdom is different from other modes of knowledge. But—you may already know, or you may soon find out—a school of theology is not that different from other kinds of schools. Sometimes a school of theology can feel like something of a bait and switch. Our website can read like Wisdom's call: "Come to me, and learn noble things, real things, things of a higher order. Come to me, and know the God who longs to be known. Come to me, and learn Who." But then you come—we come (for your faculty want this no less than you do)—and we find ourselves learning that the Council of Nicaea was convened in 325 (I mean the first council of course—we also learn that there were others). We find ourselves learning how to offer care that gives life, or at least does less harm. We find ourselves learning why baptism matters. These are all good things, vital things. But they still work at the level of knowing that, knowing how, and knowing why. And we come here because we want to know who.

If Wisdom is so different, of another order, why is a school dedicated to Holy Wisdom not also of another order? Where is knowing who on the syllabus? Or, as the cry will go up in a couple of weeks, as it does every year, right around the midterm in the Old Testament intro class: why am I flipping flashcards when I really just want to love the Lord?

The school is not of another order because we—all of us—are not of another order. And because we are not of another order, even when we dedicate ourselves to teaching and learning who, we end up teaching and learning that, and how, and why.

Let me show you what I mean. When we try to teach who God is, we often end up teaching that God is three in one, that God keeps covenant, that God does not let death have the last word. We believe these things. We stake our lives on them. They are worth teaching and learning. But there is all the difference in the world between knowing about God, and knowing God.

At other times when we try to teach who God is, we end up teaching how to meet God or work with God. We teach practices of prayer, worship, preaching, care, leadership. These, too, are good things, things that matter. But there is still a gap between knowing how to respond to God and knowing God.

At still other times we try to teach who God is and end up teaching why we should act in ways that yearn for God's reign on earth as it is in heaven. This, too, is good and important. This, too, is worth our lives. But there is still a gap between knowing why we should live faithful lives and knowing the God who is the source of all life.

Our attempts to know who God is end up slipping into different kinds of knowing that, knowing how, and knowing why. You can date this fall to vague powers like "the Sixties" or "the Enlightenment" or "the Reformation" or "Constantinianism" or "the Axial Age." Or you can pin it more specifically on Derrida, Kant, Luther, Scotus, Paul, Socrates, Moses, Adam and Eve ... and you could get yourself a fancy footnote for any of these. Blame whomever you will, but it does not change the fact of where we are now. Even when we teachers want students to know who God is, we end up teaching that, teaching how, teaching why. And even when we students want to learn who God is, we find ourselves learning that, learning how, and learning why. We want to meet the living God, and we find ourselves flipping flashcards and practicing techniques.

The hard truth facing every school of theology is that we cannot teach or learn directly—by our own powers—the kind of knowledge that we believe is most important. But the good news is that our coming to know God does not depend on our efforts, but on God's desire to be known. Wisdom calls us and claims us and marks us and makes us. This does not mean that our efforts at teaching and learning are useless. It just means that they are not techniques that achieve the goal of knowing God, but offerings that respond to the God who makes Godself known to us in love.

And because God longs to be known, God comes to us where we are, even in a school of theology. Wisdom does not hide away in a purified sanctuary that can be approached only through perfect pedagogy. She stands at the gates. She is at the crossroads. She comes to us in the hurly-burly of our days. Jesus calls us o'er the tumult of our life's wild restless sea. Like a great tree root Wisdom pushes up through the paved sidewalks of our syllabi. She meets us at the limits of our knowing that, in the gaps between knowing how and knowing why. If we ascend to the pinnacle of the Friday Eucharist service, God knows us there. If we make our beds in the depths of a study carrel, God knows us there. If we take the wings of the morning, and fly to a women's prison on the south side of town ... even there God's hand shall lead us. Wisdom will be known. By the grace of God, Wisdom will be known.

# CROSSCURRENTS

## TEACHING TOWARD THE PRACTICE OF MINISTRY TODAY

Christian Scharen

## I

Conrad Cherry's outstanding history of university-related divinity schools, Hurrying Toward Zion, highlights a major tension running through the center of many theological schools today.[1] The move to place theological education in the context of the university (or in the case of denominational seminaries, to imitate university-like patterns of organization) meant a durable tension emerged between theory and practice, between the aims of the academy and of the church. While individual schools have grappled with this tension in many different ways, the dominant story Cherry tells (echoed by many other works on theological education) is the overwhelming power of the academic paradigm in shaping both faculty careers and seminary curricula. The addition of fieldwork or contextual education was envisioned as a counterweight to the textual and intellectual leaning of the "classical disciplines." Yet both its structure and leadership were too often adjunct.

Over the past decade, I have worked with colleagues on a longitudinal study of learning ministry. Called the Learning Pastoral Imagination Project, it is centered on following a cohort of fifty graduates from ten seminaries as they transition into ministry careers.[2] Pastoral leadership today, we argue, requires collaboration, risk, discernment, judgment, and resilience, among other things. It requires, we think, something like what Craig Dykstra has called "pastoral imagination."[3] What is pastoral imagination? Dykstra's concept encompasses multiple intelligences which, when tutored in the day-to-day practice of ministry, yield the ability to perceive the fullness or holy depth of a person, a moment, or a situation. We have extended this understanding by drawing upon the notion of phronesis, which is practical knowledge and judgment derived from experience in practice over time. Through connecting phronesis with the gifts and work of the Holy Spirit, we argue, pastoral imagination emerges as an integrative, embodied, and relational capacity.[4]

Diverse in many ways, nonetheless our study participants tell us stories with some remarkable similarities as they describe their preparation for and beginnings in ministry. One in particular, the subject of this brief paper, relates to the kind of teaching and learning they describe as most helpful in their preparation for ministry. When asked the simple question, "What prepared you for ministry?" they tell stories about congregational internships, clinical pastoral education, and other immersion experiences. And they tell stories about the influential teachers who help them navigate these experiences as they enter into the practice of ministry. It is striking, I think, that consistently these diverse seminary graduates name as crucial what many seminaries treat as adjunct.

## II

In ATS alumni surveys, an unsurprising fact is that in looking back on their seminary experiences, seminary graduates say their teachers are far and away the most important feature of their education.[5] Our research project sheds additional light on this, helping to highlight some key aspects of why and how faculty are so crucial to student learning. We have found that immersion experiences are the most formative for learning pastoral imagination. Relatedly, we have found that those teachers who straddle classroom and context—and who help to put their subject in the context of the whole practice of ministry today—are regularly spoken of as the most influential.[6] David Perkins writes of the importance of teachers teaching "little versions of the whole game" so students can see how the specific topics in a class make sense in relation to the whole. For most seminary students, this "whole game" is the practice of ministry in its many forms.[7]

In the case of those going into ministry careers, such teaching toward the whole is crucial for creating the context for risking leadership in practice. A twenty-something student at a Midwestern denominational seminary, Eve told us how her Clinical Pastoral Education (CPE) supervisor and peer group both provided her support in debriefing—and learning from—a complex situation she faced helping a family with the death of their husband and father. "CPE," Eve comments, "was a place where some really good learning was able to grow legs." Her colloquial and bodily metaphor is apt: The experiential learning patterns of CPE, rooted in ministry practice with support for reflective engagement with that practice, helped her integrate and put into use all she had been learning in seminary thus far. Further, it helped her claim her nascent pastoral identity, letting her articulate the "grace and gravity" of pastoral ministry. She could risk putting into practice pieces of her learning and be supported in seeing how they fit into a larger whole she now was taking on in her role as minister.

Yet such teaching of the "whole game" need not only happen in field education settings, even if does so there in the most formative ways. Even traditional faculty like the Hebrew Bible professor she described to us—can engage a class both for and as ministry. While this professor had served as a pastor for a few years after seminary, his forty-year seminary career was marked by more traditional faculty work: teaching and scholarship. Yet as she recalled his course on God and Human Suffering, she described a course designed as a Bible course for ministry, literally serving as a bridge between the scholarly concerns of the bible and the existential concerns of ministry experience. Theological case studies allowed students to practice in class the sort of contextual, integrated knowing most needed for ministry. Further, Eve reported, his presence in class seemed to her offered as ministry. She noted that his pastoral bearing in class, especially in the face of student disagreements, modeled for her the kind of ministry leadership she herself tried to embody in her early years of pastoral leadership.

III

A young Mennonite pastor, Naomi has held a number of ministry roles since graduation, but—because she is a partnered lesbian—has had limited options for pastoral leadership in Mennonite congregations.[8] She currently works as a community organizer on a poverty project while serving as a part-time interim pastor in a small UCC congregation. For

Naomi, learning pastoral imagination has greatly benefited from the influence of what we are calling "teaching toward the practice of ministry." Her experience with several teachers helps to show some of the variety of persons we include in this category, and what roles they play over time.

Naomi chose Vanderbilt, a liberal university-related divinity school, after learning on a campus visit that her denominational seminary would not grant an M.Div. if she were "out and in a relationship." Despite the complicated relationship she has to her own denomination because of the restrictive policy on same-sex pastors, she is deeply committed to other aspects of its theology, including its strong focus on Jesus' nonviolence in the face of the powers of this world. She tells of attending a national Mennonite convention in college where, in the midst of thousands singing in four-part harmony, she experienced a deep sense of call to ministry.

Early on at divinity school, Naomi shared her hopes with her advisor, L., a history professor, and with M., a professor of the practice of ministry who directs the field education programs. Upon hearing her plans, L. said "you're not the first lesbian to sit here and tell me that." She advised that for most people it doesn't work out, and so Naomi had best have a backup plan. Naomi, while appreciating the realism, was not ready to close off the search. M. heard her deep sense of call and then worked with her to find three nationally prominent Mennonite churches known for publicly welcoming GLBTQ persons. Together, they crafted letters to each asking about a summer pastoral internship for a gay Mennonite student. After a phone interview with a Pacific Northwest congregation, and a positive congregational meeting, the plan was set.

M. was not only a caring and effective advocate for Naomi's goals, but also impacted her by the action/reflection methodology of a required second-year course in supervised ministry. Most theological schools have some version of this familiar experiential learning component as part of their curriculum: a field education placement in congregations or faith-based nonprofits, combined with required structured time for reflection. Naomi and the other four ministers in our study from Vanderbilt all remarked about the durable impact of their particular formation in this process. Based on a case-study model of theological reflection, students are asked to engage three aspects of a given situation: doing, being, and thinking.[9] Doing focuses on skills and competences, being acknowledges the importance of presence and identity, and thinking refers to the importance of wrestling with theological issues.

Reflecting on the impact on her ministry practice, Naomi recalled a crisis at the UCC church where she served as youth pastor after graduation. The senior pastor's 18-year-old son was in a terrible accident and suffered a major brain injury. He had grown up in the congregation and was loved by all. Most of the congregation would not yet know of the accident as they gathered for church that Sunday morning. Naomi stepped in to lead worship, and planned to tell the congregation right away, since the absence of the senior pastor would be obvious. She had prepared a special time of prayer, thinking through how to lead in the most helpful way. She said:

I took the field education model that we used, so the doing and being and the thinking of ministry and so I took the doing and the being, those two components and I said, "We all want to do something. We want to rage at this senseless accident. We want to fix things for Joy, but our challenge and our call at this time is just to be." That really connected with the people because no one knew what to do. What ended up happening, we had a meaningful time of prayer.

Naomi also shared about using this same reflective practice framework for her youth leadership. "We go and do a service project and then take time to reflect and that's really intentional." She'll often pose a question, like "Where did you see Jesus today?" Asked what the kids say, she laughed and said "all kinds of things-like 'I didn't see Jesus anywhere'." Yet even joking answers are effective, she said, because "the model itself is doing the work." As Naomi shared these stories, the other four graduates from her school chimed in with their own examples. The experiential learning framework taught by M. in the field education courses was formative and serves as both pattern of and resource for their ministry.

## IV

Naomi also found W., her congregational internship supervisor, to be an incredible teacher and mentor both during her seminary experience and after. It is true that most field education experience, like Naomi's, require some sort of supervisory sessions to reflect on ministry practice. While these teachers are not faculty, from the student perspective they can be powerfully influential exactly because they guide the student's first leap into leadership in ministry. They are, as David Perkins puts it, guides to the "whole game." Naomi recalls:

> The day we met, W. planned to orient me to the church, a repurposed movie theater in the middle of a busy northeast Seattle neighborhood. We got out of the car and were headed toward the offices with a full agenda: meet staff, tour building, set-up office space, when a homeless couple approached. Clearly W. had spent a good deal of time with the two, who I later learned made their home in the blocks around the church. "Pastor, will you pray with us?" they asked. And so we did. This was my first lesson: Pay attention to the interruptions.

She remarked that W. made space for her to join into the fullness of the role, walking alongside her and reflecting on her experience as she tried out ministry. She recalled:

> I got to preach and lead worship and planned worship and attended meetings and hung out with people and had coffee and went to their regional meetings. And so, and I thought "Well, I can do this. This is something I'm suited for-the rhythm of a pastoral ministry ..."

W. created space and safety to risk trying many new things, something Jean Lave and Etienne Wenger, in their discussion of apprenticeship call "legitimate peripheral participation."[10] Partly this means a kind of withdrawal, making space in the roles he usually inhabits for her to step in and try out her own voice and leadership. Yet his relational credibility and spiritual authority in community extend to her, allowing her nascent leadership to be received as one with authority she has not yet earned. Further, the dialectic of action and reflection gives ample space for articulating the wisdom embedded in practice, a special gift of these teacher/practitioners.[11] One of the most important elements in the transition from imagining ministry to embodying pastoral imagination is just this space to risk being a minister in all its complexity, and saying, often with delight and some surprise, "Well, I can do this!"

## V

When students do not have the benefit of such apprenticeship—and especially during immersion experiences where people "try on" a new ministerial identity—they experience complications in the process of learning pastoral imagination. Two brief examples from the group we are following from a large Southern Evangelical seminary help show the kinds of challenges faced by students when things don't go well. For some, like Jim, these complications cause grief and hardship along the way, but do not ultimately derail a vocation in ministry altogether. For others, like Mariana, the harsh experience of rejection has contributed to following other vocational paths instead of ministry leadership.

Jim, born and raised in a church-going Southern Baptist, describes himself as a "golden boy." Active in his church youth group, the youth pastor picked Jim out for leadership roles leading to a call to ministry. In college, he was student body president—respected and with a sense of idealism about church and the life of faith.

He married his college sweetheart and, after graduation, took a ministry internship job in a large Baptist church in another state. His role was to start a new "next-generation" service. With little support and high expectations, complicated by a disagreement over theology and mission with the senior pastor, Jim floundered. He recalls a low point in the pastor's office:

> He told me that when he hired me he expected me to be happy and loyal and I was being neither right now and I, I looked back at him and I said "When you hired me, you said you were going to be a mentor and you were going to teach me things, and you haven't done crap."

The story doesn't end tragically, however. Jim quit, but continued at the church, and in a heart to heart with God, heard a voice say, "I didn't tell you to leave." In fact, he disrespected leaders who quit when the going got tough. He went back to his senior pastor, asked for his job back, and got a second chance. Things healed, and he was able to see the pastor with respect, turning to him for advice. Yet, he admits, "I kind of had to make a part of myself die in order to be there ... I had to learn to support his system, as opposed to doing mine." After three years, Jim's desire for another level of authority and leadership led to his decision to leave and return to seminary. He now serves as pastor of a Baptist church in North Carolina.

Mariana, a student in the same cohort as Jim, had a quite different experience in her pastoral internship. Her words tell the story of what happened to her and her husband:

> We went to work in the city where I went to college ... We decided to work with a very poor church in a very urban setting. They did a lot of work with homeless and prostitutes and drug addicts so we thought that was going to be interesting. We got there and the pastor was completely against me and J. didn't know how to speak Portuguese then so I had to be involved in everything and translate, and the pastor wouldn't talk to me. He would talk to my husband. and I had to translate and that was hard because when I left Brazil to come here to go to seminary it was because in Brazil I couldn't go, so I went to seminary kind of in a dilemma because I felt the call but I didn't understand how could I be called if I was a woman. It didn't make sense. Then I went to seminary and realized I can do this, you know, women are called too, but then whenever I went into the field, I wasn't accepted in the church where we were working, the pastor would invite J. to come preach and go visit people in the hospital and go to the prison with him and I couldn't do anything, not even go with him. They wouldn't let me. The only thing they would let me do was, it's a very poor church and it's tile; you know, so once a week I was allowed to go there and wash the church, like literally wash the walls, the floor, all the chairs, wash the bathrooms, which I actually enjoyed, (chuckle) I mean, you know, I wasn't able to do anything so at least while I was there it was like I might just be washing the bathroom but at least it's still the house of the Lord.

Ada María Isasi-Díaz argues a key challenge facing Latina Women is "invisible invisibility."[12] The phrase refers to the experience of being ignored by those who do not even recognize the reality of the destructive contempt they inhabit. Through Mariana's powerful story of non-recognition in her calling, we can grasp some sense of what Isasi-Díaz means by the phrase "invisible invisibility." Despite entertaining doubts about the value of theological study affirming her sense of calling when she is so utterly rejected by the church she trained to serve, washing the bathroom can be for Mariana tenaciously redeemed as a way to serve the Lord, and as a potentially prophetic symbol of her hope to serve more fully. While consigned to clean the church as a mode of silencing, Mariana attempts to reframe the experience as part of her struggle not only to find her voice, but a place to serve in ministry. Complications like Mariana's don't allow some who are called to ministry, often women, to take the full plunge into the daily practice of ministry. She and others make the most of their situation, but the conditions themselves can slow or prevent the budding and growth of pastoral imagination.

## VI

In its classical academic form, theological education over the past hundred years has modeled itself on a textual paradigm, focused on practices of teaching and learning in classrooms. Our research adds its voice to a growing chorus calling for a shift to a contextual paradigm we believe most powerfully aids learning pastoral imagination. Such a paradigm does not simply highlight the crucial role of contextual education as a part of theological education. Rather, it would flip the center and margins, making contexts of ministry practice central with reflective learning across a range of topics adjunct to them. Many leaders and much literature have called for some version of this transformation in theological education.[13] Yet, as Conrad Cherry points out, such insight rarely was carried through "to a restructuring of programs of study" and the "classical disciplines still constituted the core of a curriculum aimed at the production of students equipped with the latest technical scholarship ..."[14] Experiments of many sorts have been tried or are currently underway which embody something of this paradigm shift, and I am a curious observer, seeking to understand what works, how, and why.

## Notes

1. Conrad Cherry, *Hurrying Toward Zion* (Bloomington, IN: Indiana University Press, 1995), especially chapters four and five, 127-82.
2. For an overview of the study and its early findings, see especially Christian Scharen and Eileen Campbell-Reed, *Learning Pastoral Imagination: A Five-Year Report on How New Ministers Learn in Practice*, Auburn Studies 21 (Winter 2016); see also Eileen Campbell-Reed and Christian Scharen, "'Holy Cow, This Stuff is Real!': From Imagining Ministry to Pastoral Imagination." *Teaching Theology and Religion* (October 2011): 323-42.
3. See his fullest statement here: Craig Dykstra, "Pastoral and Ecclesial Imagination," 41-61 in Dorothy Bass and Craig Dykstra, *For Life Abundant: Practical Theology, Theological Education,*

*and Christian Ministry* (Grand Rapids, MI: Eerdmans, 2008). Our deeper discussion of the capacity is here: Eileen Campbell-Reed and Christian Scharen, "The Unfolding of Pastoral Imagination" in *Reflective Practice: Formation and Supervision in Ministry* 32:101-17.

4. We follow Kathleen Cahalan here who, in her book *Introducing the Practice of Ministry* (Collegeville, PA: The Liturgical Press, 2010), XX, expands pastoral imagination in relation to phronesis and the gifts of the Holy Spirit undergirding the wise practice of ministry.

5. ATS Alumni survey data.

6. This finding is corroborated by Tony Wagner's work *Creating Innovators: The Making of Young People Who Will Change the World* (New York: Scribner, 2012). For the young twenty or thirty-something innovators Wagner interviewed, the most influential teachers (usually from the college years) had one foot in the academic world and one foot in practice. Almost all were non-tenured faculty, existing in marginal positions of power and influence. Their own institutions typically do not value teachers who focus on practice as highly as those doing theoretical research and academic writing, more traditional measures for tenure and scholarly prestige. Similar dynamics are at play in theological education.

7. David Perkins, 2009, *Making Learning Whole: How Seven Principles of Teaching Can Transform Education*, San Francisco, CA: Jossey-Bass.

8. Mennonites generally have been reluctant to change policy on same-sex pastors. See Michael A. King, 2009, *Stumbling Towards a Genuine Conversation on Homosexuality*, Telford, PA: Cascadia.

9. In addition to spending 10 hours a week at a ministry placement and meeting weekly in both supervisor sessions and in a ministry seminar, students write case studies based upon situations that arise in their daily work. They write three case studies per semester, discussing them both with their supervisor and with the seminar.

10. *Situated Learning: Legitimate Peripheral Participation* (New York: Cambridge University Press, 1991).

11. See Patricia Benner, 1994, "The Role of Articulation in Understanding Practice and Experience as Sources of Knowledge in Clinical Nursing," in James Tully and Daniel Weinstock, eds., *Philosophy in an Age of Pluralism: The Philosophy of Charles Taylor in Question*, Cambridge: Cambridge University Press, pp. 136-55.

12. Ada María Isasi-Díaz, in her book *En La Lucha/In The Struggle: Elaborating a Mujerista Theology* (Minneapolis, MN: Augsburg Fortress, 1993), 188.

13. See here the recent report on theological field education making just this case: Christian Scharen and Sharon Miller, *Making Theology Matter: Field Education as the Practical-Prophetic Heart of Effective Ministry Preparation*, Auburn Studies 24 (Fall 2018).

14. Cherry, *Hurrying Toward Zion*, 181.

# CROSSCURRENTS

## IDENTITY QUESTS, INDEBTED DIVERSITIES, AND SERVING "THE CHURCH": LIVING THE QUESTIONS OF MINISTERIAL FORMATION

C. Melissa Snarr

As a Christian social ethicist, I most often begin analysis with a scan of the institutions in a particular social ecology. What's there? In what organizational forms? What are their primary practices? How do they form persons' and communities' moral/political/spiritual agency? Whose forming whom? For what end? And how is necessary accountability and resistance also fostered?

Yet this essay is not a grand Dan Aleshire-style piece that maps the landscape of theological education or even theological schools. Rather this is small reflection on the institution in which I have worked for the whole of my post-doctoral career. I spiral out from Vanderbilt Divinity School (VDS) in this essay because I think some of the key challenges of the changing U.S. religious landscape are embodied at this non-denominational, historically progressive, university-related Divinity School where we are very much "between the times." We may not be the canary in the coalmine, but climate change is certainly challenging our nesting and migration patterns. In what follows, I explore key questions related to this context: the decline of denominational identity, rise of religious nones, increased diversity, vocational expansion, and doctoral training. I conclude by noting what leadership qualities might also be needed "between the times."

### The denominational identity quest

While VDS has always been denominationally diverse, we have seen a consistent decline of denominational identity in applications to the school over the last ten years. Our admissions' demographics actually track the overall decline in denominational identity and loyalty in the United States as a whole. Yet surprisingly, our MDiv graduates have a higher rate of denominational affiliation than our matriculants. In other words, our students are more likely to gain (or revive) a denominational identity while they sojourn with us. When we begin to recognize that theology schools are now often places to discern denominational identity, how does/should this change our understanding of formation for congregational ministry? Two of the students in my recent Sr. Seminar are planting churches for the Disciples of Christ (one a progressive rural church, the other in a medium security prison). Yet, they've both have been Disciples of Christ for less than two years. Is that the hopeful future of denominational renewal or is it further concern for the crisis of denominational identity? Simultaneously, some denominations are pulling certifications from theology schools which are not denominational enough. In what ways can we take denominational formations seriously while offering the flexibility for discernment and ecumenical formation that is the reality for growing numbers of persons in the United States?

**Formation and religious nones**

Intertwined with the question of denominational loyalty is the rapid rise of religious "nones." While United Methodists are still the largest percentage of our student population, our next two affiliation categories are nondenominational and "none." Religious Nones are the third largest population in our theological classrooms and the fastest growing. Of course, identifying as religious none does not mean persons are unreligious. While indications of religious practice and belief are different, they are not absent but rather reconfigured. But three markers are quite noticeable among the religious nones we teach: (1) Their religious formations are episodic, (2) they are quite wounded by traditional ecclesial structures, and (3) many seek VDS as an alternative church. As I read through applications, I notice how discreet and time-defined experiences inform these student's religious longings and questions. Immersion in a community for a long period of time rarely stands at the center of their biographies; rather, they are sojourners who move among communities often and have intense turning points. Many of those turning points are also often woundings by ecclesial communities. As a recent application attested, "After this profound rejection in high school, I didn't find God again until my undergraduate religion classes...I want to keep finding that God at VDS." What kind of formations should theological schools provide these students? What are the risks or even possibilities of trying to be an alternative church? In what ways are we also becoming a therapeutic community? Should we be pressing these students into more sustained immersion in communities and spiritual disciplines? Or is there even more creative energy and hope in providing a sort of open architecture in which students can continue to explore a range of spiritual formations and learn the artistry of ongoing recombinations?

While these questions remain open for me, I think we are seeing the rising importance of continuing education opportunities for these kinds of religious seekers who are continually and intentionally reconstituting their "traditions." Three years and done is not enough. While many of us at University divinity schools engage our doctoral students over the course of the careers, the formal structures for doing this with our master-level alums are comparatively anemic. Moreover, our role as a liminal religious space [or even a "movement half-way house" (Aldon Morris)] may be crucial in a religious ecology where choice is appropriately prized but can also easily slide into consumerism. How do we help students navigate the path of ongoing reconstitution that is faith in a "secular age"?

**Indebted diversities**
As we reflect on these religious identity markers, VDS also recognizes that they are bound up with the growing diversity in terms of gender/gender expression, race/ethnicity, nationality, and sexuality orientation. While we are not as racially diverse as some of our independent seminary colleagues, Association of Theological Schools (ATS) institutions are the most demographically diverse they have ever been in terms of gender and race/ethnicity. While ATS will not gather data on how many students identify as gay, lesbian, bisexual, or queer, VDS has been gathering that data for the past several years (and would invite others to add voluntarily this question to their ATS student questionnaires). In the last several years, between 9 percent and 22 percent of our graduates identified as LGBQ. These kinds of shifts challenge theological schools to move beyond tolerance to deep engagement and collaboration across difference;

our curriculums and student life must work hard and intentionally to lead rather than follow the trends. These demographic shifts also mean starting vocational development programs about "when/how to come out in your ordination process," "breaking the gendered associate minister ceiling," and "navigating cross-cultural appointments."

These are wonderful challenges. But in this midst of these shifts, I am quite worried about how increases in student indebtedness track most decidedly along racial/ethnic lines and are compounded by non-mainline identification. This trend is also not significantly reduced even with higher tuition awards. At what point do we turn away students who are already carrying $40–50,000 in debt into their theological studies? In what ways can we actually counter the raced dynamics of wealth inequality for a large segment of our students?

Finally, we continue to be uncomfortable with whether to admit international students who have strong seminaries in their home countries either for their first and, especially, their second theological degrees. At what point does this enforce neo-colonialism and continue a brain drain from these countries? What do we offer them that is essential to their education? Is this a short-term strategy that largely benefits the diversity of our classrooms and bottom lines?

**Serving "the church"?**
All of these shifts in demographics (denominational identity, religious nones, gender/race/sexuality) also intersect a rise in the range of vocational trajectories for our students. While enrollment in our M.Div. program remains relatively high compared to other ATS schools, only about 40 percent of our MDiv students go on to congregational ministry. Almost all of our MTS students and the remainder of our MDivs go on to pursue myriad types of employment. And not because they cannot find a congregation; rather, ministry has a wider definition for these students. Certainly, some will go on to doctoral work or law school, but a large swath of our students end up in various forms of chaplaincy, non-profits, community organizing, social enterprises, or even the military and business sectors. At any one time in our classrooms, we cannot assume the congregational trajectory is the dominant one for our students. In recent conversation with a dean at Fuller Seminary (not a school we normally think of as similar to VDS), I was surprised how similar our range of employment

trajectories was and how Fuller was also working to expand the nature of their curriculum. This phenomenon presses us to expand our understanding of religious leadership development, organizational dynamics, and ministerial imagination. But these areas push beyond faculty competencies even in traditional ministerial arts such as homiletics, liturgics, education, missions, and congregational leadership. How do uphold our academic standards when stretching into new competency areas? In what ways can we expand our vision and context for ministry while not neglecting congregations? And in light of these shifts, what does it mean to be accountable or in service to "the church"?

**Doctoral technique**
All of these questions about educating for ministry also intertwine with Vanderbilt's role in the training of doctoral students. While our Lilly-funded Theology and Practice program attempts explicitly to form doctoral students who are leaders in their disciplines and in the training of ministers, we continue to hear deep concerns from our seminary colleagues about preparation for seminary teaching. The structure of disciplines does not easily serve the complex navigations of ministerial leadership. How do we take this seriously while also recognizing the need and importance for the generative, seemingly "irrelevant" space of the academy? How immediate should our push for seminary style relevance be with our doctoral students? When does this doctoral education become hostage to practical technique? I ask these questions in part because my own disposition and field of ethics tend toward the more immediately relevant. But I also recognize the vital contributions of colleagues in more classical disciplines that may not have as immediate and felt practical import. In what ways can we hold on to multiple goods and still have a vital doctoral program?

**Living the questions with ministerial imagination**
All these questions are not hard to ask, and there are even more that we could pose (financial modeling, interfaith education, etc.). Obviously, most are hard to answer. As an administrative leader at a theological school, I sometimes wish they would answer themselves or at least go away for a while. But there is a dual temptation that is great for theological faculties and leaders: (1) avoiding the questions and (2) thinking we have them

neatly answered. The first isolates us from our students, our communities, each other, and ultimately—I contend—our Living God. This is the journey of faith, and faith requires asking what God is doing in this time and how we respond fittingly. The second underestimates the complexity of the questions, our students, our communities, and perhaps God, while overestimating our capacities.

Instead, I think leadership in at this moment requires living these questions openly with our colleagues, across institutions, and taking fitting risks knowing, from the outset, that we will need courage and humility for continual revision. These are times for honesty and encouragement of a kind of creativity that balances the strength of traditional models with vital experimentations while embracing a robust theology of risk and even failure. Leadership in theological education will require much of what we hope for in ministerial imagination: contextual sensitivity, relational trust, habits of justice and inclusion, traditioned insight, wise risk, and spiritual depth. Perhaps as we reflect more on the formation for the necessary flux of ministerial imagination, we can also begin to have a more sure footing in how we live the tough but generative questions of theological education at theological schools.

# CROSSCURRENTS

## WHY GAMES AND GAMING MIGHT BE THE BEST WAY AND PLACE IN WHICH TO CONSIDER THE MEANING AND PURPOSES OF THEOLOGICAL EDUCATION
A Reflection

Mary E. Hess

For the last fifteen years, I have been on the faculty of an ELCA seminary in the upper Midwest. At the same time, I have been a very active lay member of a local Roman Catholic community. This is the "situatedness" from which I reflect in this essay, and these are the places and experiences which give me passion for the work of theological education. My research and writing have focused on shaping faith and learning in the midst of digital cultures, and during that time period I have watched as digitally mediated spaces have moved from being something only young people inhabit, to a ubiquitous part of everyday life for nearly everyone in the United States, let alone in other spaces around the globe.

There is no longer any way to remain "offline" entirely—people without ready access to the net find themselves without access to a whole host of basic necessary infrastructure, everything from phone numbers (phone books having gone the way of VHS tapes), to employment (the vast majority of job applications require some form of online access), to government electronic benefits (access to SNAP, health exchanges, unemployment benefits, and so on, is primarily online), and so on.[1]

I have written at length elsewhere about specific challenges to theological education that arise from these dynamics, and noted both resources and dilemmas that exist in the midst of learning with these spaces.² Here, I want to take a turn that might appear to many readers to be audacious to the point of irrelevance, or perhaps whimsical to the point of the trivial. In what follows, I invite you to consider what we, that is theological educators and theological education, might have to learn from game design and gaming communities.

Why game design and gaming? Perhaps statistics such as these offer one reason

1. Sixty-nine percent of all heads of household play computer and video games.
2. Ninety-seven percent of youth play computer and video games.
3. Forty percent of all gamers are women.
4. One out of four gamers are over the age of fifty.
5. The average game player is thirty-five years old and has been playing for twelve years.
6. Most gamers expect to continue playing games for the rest of their lives.³

Compare that with Pew's data, which suggests that less than half of millennials attend church regularly, and fully one in four adults under age 30 are "unaffiliated" with any religion.⁴

When an entire generation of people find themselves drawn into games, and when digital video makes games immediately accessible in one's personal space while yet having global reach and possibility, it is worth paying attention. Jane McGonigal, one of the key scholars in this arena, has written a best-selling book entitled *Reality is Broken: Why Games Make Us Better and How They Can Change the World*. This is the book that woke me up to the possibilities and that challenged me to set aside at least some of my own skepticism to enter her argument.

She writes, for example, that:

> We can no longer afford to view games as separate from our real lives and our real work. It is not only a waste of the potential of games to do real good—it is simply untrue. Games don't distract us from our real lives. They fill our real lives: with positive emotions, positive activity, positive experiences, and positive strengths. Games aren't leading us to the downfall of human civilization. They're leading us to its reinvention. The great challenge for us today, and for the remainder of the century, is to integrate games more closely

into our everyday lives, and to embrace them as a platform for collaborating on our most important planetary efforts. If we commit to harnessing the power of games for real happiness and real change, then a better reality is more than possible—it is likely. And in that case, our future together will be quite extraordinary.[5]

I can perhaps sense some of your responses to her words, given how often I have heard them from other people: "surely it's not appropriate simply to give people what they want?" "isn't her claim that 'reality is broken' a reason to run away from digital games, rather than toward them?" "wouldn't this mean that theological education would become a consumer-led tar pit, rather than a prophetic spring of refreshing water?" "there can't possibly be anything remotely generative, not theologically at least, about digital games!" These are some of the more polite responses I have heard. But the more I talk with people who are deeply involved in digital games, particularly alternative reality games, the more I have become convinced that there is something important occurring there.

There is quite a lot of research, for instance, that notes the ways in which playing games can increase cognitive capacity, support pro-social behavior, elicit wonder in the face of difference (rather than resistance), improve mindfulness, and so on.[6] The MacArthur Foundation has funded a decade's worth of such research and compiled it into a series of quite persuasive books engaging K12 educational contexts.[7] But what about graduate education? And particularly graduate education in a theological context, pursuing theological and biblical ideas, and seeking to educate pastoral leaders?

I have often been asked, "what is theological about games?" At this point, my answer is "quite possibly everything!" Consider McGonigal's answers to the question "what are gamers virtuosos at?" She highlights four dynamics:
1. Urgent optimism
2. Social fabric (weaving a tight fabric)
3. Blissful productivity (optimized to do hard meaningful work)
4. Epic meaning[8]

Let's consider each of these in turn for their theological relevance. How much more urgent can optimism be, for example, than an optimism that can see the "already not yet" in the midst of global despair? An optimism which argues that God turns upside down all the power structures that we see in the world? How much more urgent an optimism, than one which confesses that God "knit me together in my mother's womb?" (Psalm 139) and asserts "Notice how the flowers grow. They do not toil or spin. But I tell you, not even Solomon in all his splendor was dressed like one of them" (Luke 12:27). Or confesses an understanding that death is not final, that we are baptized into death precisely because we are thus drawn into eternal life?

Or what about social fabric? Imagine how tight a social fabric is being woven in a community that values the widow, the orphan, the immigrant, and the child. Or that understands that those who mourn, those who are weak, those who hunger and thirst for righteousness must be at the center of our concern? That tight social fabric begins to be woven in the Hebrew Bible with a commitment to justice that is not so much about weak notions of fairness, but rather strong notions of right relationship, not of justice as judgment but justice as deep and holistic relationship. We hear it in Hannah's song (1 Sam 2:1-10), and it echoes again in Mary's joyful song to Elizabeth in the Magnificat (Luke 1:46-55), "God has thrown down the rulers from their thrones, but lifted up the lowly. The hungry he has filled with good things; the rich he has sent away empty."

When it comes to a notion of "blissful productivity, optimized to do hard meaningful work"—the nagging suspicion that the "Protestant work ethic" is a bleak way to be in the world can be replaced by Frederick Buechner's affirmation that vocation is where your deep joy and the world's deep needs intersect.[9] Blissful productivity can be understood as woven deeply into what we mean by vocation if we understood that word holistically. I believe that blissful productivity can be described as a heartfelt response to God's grace poured out into the world, and a hope and care that extends beyond what can reasonably be imagined to be possible.

Blissful productivity is also clearly in evidence in the ways in which children throw themselves into games—for that matter, into all that they do. What glorious blissful productivity can be observed in watching young children learn as they play! That's their job, to learn all that they can, to soak up all that is around them, and to immerse themselves in figuring out who they are. I can't help calling to mind, then, those stories in Matthew (19:14) and Luke (18:16) where Jesus admonishes his disciples and urges them "to let the little children come to him," and reminds them that they need to become like children to enter the Kingdom of God.

Finally, epic meaning. Honestly, I'm not sure I can imagine a story more epic than that of God's relationship with God's people over eons. The creation story itself is epic, and the ongoing story of Eve and Adam, of the human family, of the Tower of Babel, the flood, the exodus, Daniel, David, Jonah, Ruth and Naomi, Hannah and Sarah, the prophets, all the way up through the community of outsiders following Jesus, into our very lives today.

McGonigal argues that these four factors—urgent optimism, weaving a tight social fabric, blissful productivity optimized to do hard meaningful work, and epic meaning—together build super empowered hopeful individuals. I know there have been points in time when that has been true for those who name themselves followers of the Christ. But I'm not so sure it's true now? At least not so much in North America? Certainly, theological educators and administrators of theological schools rarely claim to be "super empowered and hopeful." Which is partly why I think her observations about gaming are so pertinent to our work.

Where have these factors gone in our practices as Christians? Gandhi is quoted as saying that he liked the Christ, it's Christians he wasn't so fond of. I wonder how it is that a faith which once led—and certainly in other parts of the world, still leads—people into deep engagement with mending the social fabric, and with a hope and joy that transcends even the most dire circumstances—I wonder where that has gone here in large chunks of North America?

As I've read more deeply in the gaming literature, two things have occurred to me. First, that part of what is so powerful about games is that we "hold lightly" to the things we're doing there—they're "not real" in some sense, and we both worry about that with games, and we revel in it. We choose to play, and in playing we don't obsess so much with what we're doing, we simply delight in the process. Where is our playfulness in religious community? Can we learn to "hold lightly"?

I believe that our theological commitments point us in that direction, and perhaps our challenge is to reinvigorate this side of our confessions, to find a way in which we can be playful in religious community. The Lutherans I live and work with believe deeply that God's grace is so active and so present in the world that we can *lean into* it, that we can rely on God's overwhelming love to hold us, to free us into taking the risks necessary to mend the very ruptures in our social fabric that we have also produced.

Neuroscience is actually confirming something of this dynamic. There is a lot of evidence that people who believe in a transcendent God, and who are involved in religious community, have better outcomes on a lot of measures—less anxiety, more social connection, etc.[10] Perhaps there is something to attend to here. Perhaps in believing in God, and in a hope beyond death, we are able to "hold lightly" to this life. Certainly, in Buddhist thought there are a set of practices aimed at helping us not to "cling" to ephemeral realities. And in Hindu thought there is a deep conviction of the Holy in each of us—I think of the Hindu saying that "our job is not to seek for Love, but rather only to seek and find within us the barriers to Love." So perhaps playing, perhaps the joy of games, is about choosing to "hold lightly" in a way that frees us to become more deeply engaged. This is the kind of paradox of which Parker Palmer is so fond as he describes optimal learning environments.[11]

The second thing I would note about my own enjoyment of games is that there is fun to be had in the "do over" section of them—indeed, games that have turned that function off, games in which when you "die" you are done with the game, are usually not very much fun. I'm not a very good strategist at games, I just like to play my way through them multiple times until I figure out the right order in which to solve a given puzzle. I've had hours of fun, for instance, in the iPhone game "Tiny Thief," just trying possible actions over and over, or prior to that, in "Angry Birds."

What is it about being able to be freed up to explore and to experiment and to make mistakes that help us here?

Certainly, in religious community we have deep convictions about the role of repentance and forgiveness. Further, we confess that death is not the end. This is not a trivial confession, not a simple reflection of the "do overs" we explore in games, but the deeper belief that God promises us life beyond our brokenness.

There is much in Christian thought that points to honestly admitting that, as human beings, we screw up. We mess up all the time. But for every moment that "the law" of which Paul speaks in the various epistles condemns us, God's promise saves us. We are both, in the Lutheran language, *simul justus et peccata*, simultaneously saint and sinner.

So maybe there is something that games can remind us of here, too: That if we take our urgent optimism, expend it in the service of a tight social fabric, and throw ourselves into a kind of all-in productivity, we may end up not only living the "epic adventure" of which McGonigal speaks, but also living more deeply into God's mission in the world. And when we screw up, when we inevitably hurt ourselves and each other, we can rest assured in the promise of God that *love will win out in the end*.

I am convinced that we need to work against *the problems*, not against *each other*—that's the essence of what scholars like McGonigal are talking about, when they explore the power of alternate reality games, and I'm convinced that that is the essence of the Gospel as well.

I often note the changes that digital cultures have sparked by talking about three shifting dynamics: authority, authenticity, and agency.[12] We've moved from a place where institutional authorities could command our attention and automatically earn our respect, to a time in which authority has to be earned and structural roles sometimes make such trust in authority very hard to come by. Further, when we speak of authenticity it is most often in personal, even individual, terms. Certainly in middle class white culture what is perceived as "authentic" is nearly always determined by one's personal experiences. That didn't used to be the case in religious communities. All you have to do is think about how a liturgy professor defines "authentic worship" vs. how young adults might do so today, to perceive the shift. "Agency" has to do with whether you can make a difference and whether you can make something happen. Part of what the game design literature has invited me to consider are the possibilities present in games and game-making for engaging all three of these changing dynamics.[13]

When McGonigal writes about "super empowered hopeful individuals" as a kind of counterweight to Thomas Friedman's notion of "super empowered angry individuals,"[14] I believe she is talking about agency, and she's offering us concrete examples of ways in which the best of games and game-making invite us into hopeful engagement, into collaborative empowerment, into a kind of agency which can even invite a recognition of God's agency (although that is not her assertion but rather my own).

I think we have just that one simple thing to remind ourselves of, and everything else can flow from there: God chose to Incarnate as a way to carry God's promise of love and life to all of God's creation. God became flesh. And in doing so God chose the most humble, vulnerable of human beings in which to enter time and history: an infant, born in a stable.

Surely from that moment of joy, we can take both comfort and hope and carry them into the spaces of which game designers speak. There is deeply authentic joy present in games, we need to embrace that joy rather than be afraid of it, or dismissive of it. When McGonigal talks about how games help us to learn collaboration, she is inviting us to experience the kind of awe that comes from such collaboration. I love her definition of collaboration that it involves "cooperating, coordinating, and co-creating" and that people playing games get to practice shared concentration, synchronized engagement, mutual regard, and collective commitment (to which, she adds, they create reciprocal rewards).[15]

I think that this is what religious community has been about, at its best, through the centuries. Maybe it is time to think about religious practice and belief more like play, and less like burden or obligation? Maybe instead of complaining about how families are choosing to take their kids to soccer games on a Sunday morning instead of to religious education, we might ask what is drawing them to those games? And what kind of bigger, more epic, more cooperative, more collective, and more co-creating games might we draw them into, in religious community?

I do not in any way want to trivialize or ignore the brokenness of our lives together. In a world of the Ebola virus, of systemic racism manifesting itself in the deaths of Michael Brown, Eric Garner, and Tamir Rice (to name only a few), and of vast economic inequalities and violence, we must see deeply the reality we inhabit. But it is not enough to see them —we need to embrace and engage them, and we need the "emergensight"[16] of which McGonigal writes: the ability to thrive in a chaotic, collaborative environment seeking hope and *just* change. She tells numerous stories in her book of people who experience the joy of this kind of collaboration. I am convinced that this could be a profound example of the vocation of which Frederick Buechner speaks, the joy that comes from putting your gifts to use in service of meeting the world's deep needs.

We ought not to fear games or game-making, because we can trust that God will already be there. We can trust that God will meet us in our joy, and in our brokenness, and that God has promised us an epic adventure into which we can invite others.

So what is my own proposal for "theological education between the times"? I propose that we need to activate the largest and widest net of people we can, to explore what it might mean to carry faith into the future. We need to take seriously a "world without churches"[17] and begin to ask ourselves how the Spirit might continue to manifest in our midst in such a world. We need to imagine and explore as wildly and freely and playfully as we can, and *a massively multi-player online game could be just the space in which to do so.*

Consider, for instance, the set of questions that the faculty at Luther Seminary have been exploring off and on for the last decade[18]:

1. The nature and priorities of God's mission: Who is God and what is God up to in the world?

2. Luther Seminary's evangelical imagination and identity: Who is Luther Seminary? What is Luther Seminary going to be in the future?

3. Luther Seminary speaks of itself as a biblical, confessional, and missional seminary. What does that mean? Is that who we are? If so, is that what's needed at this moment in God's mission?

4. Luther Seminary has evolved into a center of learning with many educational processes and networks of teaching and learning: How multi-dimensional do we want to be? How many dimensions of learning and resourcing can we sustain?

5. Seminaries are often isolated from the consciousness and contexts of society. How do we get and stay in touch with the whole of God's world? How to we engage those who are doing ministry in that real world?

6. The prioritization of Luther Seminary's resources: What's most important? How much can Luther do at once?

7. The state of the church: How do we rightly respond to the diminishing vitality of many congregational and denominational forms? What's

happening? What's missing? What new needs are emerging? What new structures are needed?

8. Where are the existing vibrant, resilient congregations: What's faithful? What's effective? How would we know?

9. The diminishing numbers and shifting character of candidates for ministry: Who is coming to seminary? Who isn't coming? Who do we want or need in Christian public leadership?

10. The need to re-educate pastors already serving: What do existing pastors need to know and want to know to lead the church in this globalized, secularized society?

11. The changing expectations and lifestyles of students: Are our educational patterns out of sync with students' consciousness and lives? What about their new "ways of learning?"

12. The demands and stress placed on seminarians: Are our students using their time efficiently? Should students be paying for the bulk of their education? Are our students working too much?

13. Unsustainable costs: What does a faithful, effective, efficient teaching and learning center look like? How are seminary courses best taught? How are scholarship and research best accomplished and supported?

14. The future of denominational support: Can and how will ELCA church-wide and ELCA synods rework their priorities? What will this mean for how theological education is funded? What will this mean for how this seminary intersects with denominational priorities for ministerial formation and call processes?

15. The rising debt of graduates: Can we offer theological education less expensively to qualified candidates?

16. Possible reduction of ATS requirements for the M. Div. by 2012 (from 90 credits to 72): What do we think about the reduction? If it occurs, what does it mean for us?

17. Issues in the Seminary's present curricula: How and when do we address the changes needed in our curricula? What about non-credit requirements? Do we need a major curricular revision?

18. Ineffective personal, communal, and vocational leadership formation: Are we equipping healthy servant leaders? How do we get leaders ready for the challenges and stress of 21st century ministry?

19. The discoveries of high-impact, technology-supported, active learning: Can students learn better, more quickly?

20. Possible new models—congregationally based, congregationally partnered theological education—weekend seminary and others: What models make sense? Where and who are our most able "teaching congregations?" "Is a weekend seminary feasible?" Who else might be our partners in educating Christian public leaders

We have been asking these questions for years—but we have stayed almost entirely within churchly contexts—and in doing so, we have walked ourselves into a set of closed doors which we have not easily been able to open, let alone walk through. Meanwhile, hundreds of thousands if not millions of people have found ways to explore their faith outside of traditional institutional frameworks, while yet drawing on some of the same databases of Christian meaning.

What gives me hope in the midst of all of the statistics of decline? The energy and playfulness of people coming together in projects which have a shared vision for the future. What brings me to despair in the face of that hope? The reality that most of these projects have little or nothing to do with what we have traditionally understood as "communities of faith."

Communities of faith can and must be led by people gathering together—"where two or three are gathered in my name"—but increasingly those communities which persist will not necessarily be led by professionally trained clergy, but rather will grow from the energies, needs, and passions of people coming together in "networked communities" who are drawing upon diverse experiences to create "convergent practices" which "story their identities" in ways that "build authority" rather than assume it, and which stretch across "multiple sites" of engagement. These are characteristics Heidi Campbell has identified as elements of what she labels "networked religion," and they are emblematic of religious practice across multiple faith traditions.[19] They are also characteristic of what researchers are observing in many other settings and institutions as well, and are perhaps particularly visible in the midst of spaces largely defined as gaming environments.

Thus, people read Anne Lamott, for example, who is deeply steeped in a particular Christian community and Christian language, without ever entering a church. Or find themselves caught up in the novels of Diana Gabaldon and J.K. Rowling, grappling with deep questions of personal agency and community ethics, the nature of evil, and the power of hope, without ever knowing the underlying stories and symbols upon which those authors have drawn.

The experience of "convergent practices" means that people have found their way into pondering profoundly theological questions through the music of Macklemore & Ryan Lewis, The Blackeyed Peas, Jeremy Messersmith, Missy Elliott, and Hozier—all the while eschewing any connection to explicit religious traditions. The longing for making promises within community at the start of a marriage has meant that there is a large market for free and rapid ordination conferred online absent any study, and similarly, there is a growing market for grief support groups and funeral rituals which draw on claims of transcendence without any specificity of tradition.

So what ARE the things theological educators and theological education have to offer the world? What are the resources and claims which arise within religious community which might best be shared in the world as it is emerging around us? What is it that we can name, what are the symbols upon which we can draw, which can speak to experiences which otherwise have no name? or which can only be spoken of in hushed or embarrassed voices? I think a game design might help us to explore these questions and unlock the potential of religious communities in the world as it is emerging around us.

How do we "story our faith" in ways that help to resist the fierce individualism which is rapidly becoming toxic amidst broken economies and devastating climate consequences? How do we "story our faith" in ways that invite people into exploring what might be seen as esoteric to them? How do we "story our faith" in ways that invite engagement across difference? We must ask these questions in as wide and deep a set of contexts as we can find. If we are correct in believing that the more diverse the knowers, the more robust the knowing, then surely, we must be inviting not only laypeople in the communities which we serve into this conversation, but we must stretch ourselves into those spaces in which multiple generations, multiple cultures, are already gathered—that is, in gaming spaces—and we must seek and listen for the Holy Spirit in the midst of those communicative practices.[20] Let me return to the words of McGonigal which I shared at the beginning of this essay:

We can no longer afford to view games as separate from our real lives and our real work. It is not only a waste of the potential of games to do real good—it is simply untrue. Games don't distract us from our real lives. They fill our real lives: with positive emotions, positive activity, positive experiences, and positive strengths. Games aren't leading us to the downfall of human civilization. They're leading us to its reinvention. The great challenge for us today, and for the remainder of the century, is to integrate games more closely into our everyday lives and to embrace them as a platform for collaborating on our most important planetary efforts. If we commit to harnessing the power of games for real happiness and real change, then a better reality is more than possible—it is likely. And in that case, our future together will be quite extraordinary.

It is not too late for theological educators to enter into such profound play, and this may just be a path that the Holy Spirit has been inviting us into for some time.

**Notes**

1. At the same time as digital access has become all the more necessary, rates of access—particularly to high-speed broadband—have increased at a glacial pace, putting the United States at 31st in the world in terms of average download speeds and 42nd in the world for average upload speeds. This places the United States behind countries such as Estonia, Hungary, Slovakia, Uruguay, Lesotho, and Belarus. (http://theweek.com/articles/449919/american-internet-slow). My summer DMIN students from South Korea regularly complain about how slow and how expensive this access is. In the United States, we no longer have simply a "digital divide" between those who have computers and those who do not, and those who can get to the net and those who cannot; we have multiple divides which include those who have ready access to high-speed broadband and the devices necessary to benefit from it, and those who do not—and one of those separates the US from most highly developed market economies.
2. See, in particular, Hess (2014a and 2014b), as well as Hess (2005) and Hess and Brookfield (2008).
3. McGonigal, Jane (201101-20). *Reality Is Broken: Why Games Make Us Better and How They Can Change the World* (Kindle Locations 265-270). Penguin Group US. Kindle Edition. Note that she is not arguing that ALL games do this, because there are clearly some games with disastrous content and practices, but on the whole games generally accomplish these things.
4. Pew data: http://www.pewforum.org/2010/02/17/religion-among-the-millennials/
5. McGonigal, Jane (201101-20). *Reality Is Broken: Why Games Make Us Better and How They Can Change the World* (Kindle Locations 5773-5780). Penguin Group US. Kindle Edition.
6. See, for instance, Ito, *et al.* (2010), Gee (2007, 2013), Jenkins (2009), Rheingold (2012), not to mention all of the science made accessible here: http://janemcgonigal.com/learn-me/
7. See, for instance, http://www.macfound.org/programs/learning/

8. Transcript of a TED talk by Jane McGonigal in February of 2010, http://www.ted.com/talks/jane_mcgonigal_gaming_can_make_a_better_world/transcript?language=en
9. Easily accessed here: https://www.goodreads.com/quotes/140448-the-place-god-calls-you-to-is-the-place-where
10. McGonigal notes a lot of this research at her site (http://janemcgonigal.com/learn-me/), and there is a good collection of it at the Religious Education Association's 2011 meeting site (http://www.religiouseducation.net/rea2011/resource)
11. Palmer (2007), and his paradoxes of learning design.
12. See, for example, Hess (2010, 2014c, 2015).
13. See Carnes (2014), Campbell and Grieve (2014), Hoover and Emerich, eds. (2011).
14. Friedman (1999).
15. McGonigal, Jane (201101-20). *Reality Is Broken: Why Games Make Us Better and How They Can Change the World* (Kindle Location 4385). Penguin Group US. Kindle Edition.
16. Ibid.
17. Here, I am pointing to the possibility of creating a game like "world without oil" (http://en.wikipedia.org/wiki/World_Without_Oil)
18. This iteration comes from this site: https://sites.google.com/a/luthersem.edu/contemporary-consciousness-and-cultures/
19. Campbell (2012).
20. I have written elsewhere (Hess, 2014c) about how a view of the social Trinity matches up well with the "create, share, believe" form of faith emerging in the midst of digital spaces, but I would emphasize here that it is the *communicative* nature of the social Trinity which so aptly emerges in these contexts.

## Works Cited

Campbell, H., 2012, "Understanding the Relationship Between Religion Online and Offline in a Networked Society," Journal of the American Academy of Religion **80**(1), pp. 64–93.

Campbell, H., and G. Grieve, 2014, Playing With Religion in Digital Games, Bloomington, IN: Indiana University Press.

Carnes, M., 2014, Minds on Fire: How Role-Immersion Games Transform College, Cambridge, MA: Harvard University Press.

Friedman, T., 1999, The Lexus and the Olive Tree: Understanding Globalization, New York: Picador.

Gee, J., 2007, What Video Games Have to Teach us About Learning and Literacy, New York: Palgrave Macmillan.

Gee, J., 2013, The Anti-Education Era: Creating Smarter Students Through Digital Learning, New York: Palgrave Macmillan.

Hess, M., 2005, Engaging Technology in Theological Education: All That We Can't Leave Behind, New York: Rowman & Littlefield.

Hess, M., and S. Brookfield, eds., 2008, Teaching Reflectively in Theological Contexts: Promises and Contradictions. Malabar, FL: Krieger.

Hess, M., 2010, "From ICT to TCI: Communicative Theology(ies), Pedagogy and Web 2.0.," in M. Scharer, B. Hinze, and B. Hilberath, eds., KommunikativeTheologie:ZugariGe– Auseinandersetzungen– Ausdifferenzierungen, Wien: Lit Verlag GmbH & Co., pp. 130–49.

Hess, M., 2014a, "A New Culture of Learning: Digital Storytelling and Faith Formation," Dialog, **53**(1), Spring, pp. 12–22.

Hess, M., 2014b, "A New Culture of Learning: What are the Implications for Theological Educators," Teaching Theology and Religion, **17**(3), July, pp. 227–32.

Hess, M., 2014c, "And the Word Went Viral: Finding God at the Intersection of Scripture and Popular Media," America, July 21–28, 2014.

Hess, M., 2015, "Learning With Digital Technologies: Privileging Persons Over Machines," Journal of Moral Theology, **1**(4), Winter, pp. 131–50.

Hoover, S., and M. Emerich, eds., 2011, Media, Spiritualities and Social Change, London: Continuum International Publishing Group.

Ito M, Baumer S, Bittanti M, boyd d., Cody R, Herr-Stephenson B, Horst HA, Lange PG, Mahendran D, Martínez KZ, Pascoe CJ, Perkel D, Robinson L, Sims C, and Tripp L., 2010, Hanging Out, Messing Around, Geeking Out: Kids Living and Learning With New Media, Cambridge, MA: MIT Press.

Jenkins, H., 2009, Confronting the Challenges of Participatory Culture: Media Education in the 21st Century, Cambridge, MA: MIT Press.

McGonigal, J., 2011, Reality is Broken: Why Games Make Us Better and How They Can Change the World, New York: Penguin Press.

Palmer, P., 1998, The Courage to Teach: Exploring the Inner Landscape of a Teacher's Life, San Francisco, CA: Jossey-Bass.

Palmer, P., 2007, The Courage to Teach(2nd edtion), San Francisco, CA: Jossey-Bass.

Rheingold, H., 2012, Netsmart: How to Thrive Online, Cambridge, MA: MIT Press.

# CROSSCURRENTS

# CONTRIBUTORS

**Zainab Alwani** is Associate Professor and the Founding Director of Islamic Studies at the Howard University School of Divinity (HUSD). She is the chair of Master of Arts (Religious Studies) program at HUSD. She is an Islamic scholar, researcher, and community activist. Dr. Alwani is the first female jurist to serve on the board of the Fiqh Council of North America and currently serves as the Council's Vice-Chair. Her research focuses on Quranic studies, Islamic jurisprudence, the relationship between civil and religious law in the area of family and gender, and interreligious relations.

(zainab.alwani@howard.edu)

**Eileen R. Campbell-Reed** is Coordinator for Coaching, Mentoring & Internships and Associate Professor of Practical Theology at Central Baptist Theological Seminary. She is also Co-Director of the Learning Pastoral Imagination Project, an ongoing longitudinal, ecumenical, national study of learning ministry in practice. She is the author of numerous books and articles, most recently Anatomy of a Schism: How Clergywomen's Narratives Reinterpret the Fracturing of the Southern Baptist Convention (University of Tennessee Press, 2016).

(eileen@pastoralimagination.com)

**Mary E. Hess**, Professor of Educational Leadership, joined the Luther Seminary faculty in July 2000. Hess received her B.A. degree in American Studies in 1985 from Yale University in New Haven, Connecticut. She received her M.T.S. degree in 1992 from Harvard University in Cambridge, Massachusetts. In 1998, she received her Ph.D. in religion and education from Boston College in Chestnut Hill, Massachusetts. Hess' most recent professional experience includes serving on the editorial board of the premier journal in her field, Religious Education (1999-present), working with the Lexington Seminar and the Wabash Center, and serving as a core member of the International Study Commission on Media, Religion and Culture. She is a member of the Religious Education Association, the American Academy of Religion, and the Catholic Theological Society of America. Her most recent publications include the books Teaching Reflectively in Theological Contexts: Promises and Contradictions (Melbourne, FL: Krieger, 2008) and Engaging technology in theological education: All that we can't leave behind (New York: Rowman & Littlefield 2005). She maintains her own website and has written her weblog, Tensegrities, since 2003.

(mhess@luthersem.edu)

**Willie James Jennings** is Associate Professor of Systematic Theology and Africana Studies at Yale Divinity School.

His book *The Christian Imagination: Theology and the Origins of Race* (link is external) (Yale 2010) won the American Academy of Religion Award of Excellence in the Study of Religion in the Constructive-Reflective category the year after it appeared and, in 2015, the Grawemeyer Award in Religion, the largest prize for a theological work in North America. Englewood Review of Books called the work a "theological masterpiece."

(willie.jennings@yale.edu)

**vănThanh Nguyễn** is a missionary priest of the Society of the Divine Word and has served as *Professor of New Testament Studies, Advisor for the MA in Biblical Ministry, and Bishop Francis X. Ford, MM, Chair of Catholic Missiology* on the Catholic Theological Union faculty since 2005. He is the Rector (or Superior) of Divine Word Theologate located in Hyde Park, Chicago. He serves on the Board of Directors and the Board Trustees of Divine Word College (2011-present) and the Board of Directors of the American Society of Missiology (2017-present). He is a co-convener and coordinator of Biblical Studies and Mission (BISAM) in the International Association for Mission Studies (IASM; 2012-present). He is an associate editor of the *Journal of the International Association for Mission Studies* (MS; 2013-present) and the managing editor of the *Journal of Association of Asian/North American Theological Educators* (JAANATE; 2013-present).

(tnguyen@ctu.edu)

**Christian Scharen** is Vice President of Applied Research and leads of the Center for the Study of Theological Education at Auburn. His main research and writing interests center on practical theology and theological education, with a particular interest in what strengthens leaders of faith and moral courage in facing the challenges of justice, peace, and equity in the twenty-first century. A leading scholar working at the intersection of social science and theology, he lectures and writes in the areas of innovation and change in theological education and social change leadership of faith communities today. Scharen is Co-Director of the Learning Pastoral Imagination Project, an ongoing longitudinal, ecumenical, national study of learning ministry in practice.

(cscharen@auburnseminary.org)

**Ted A. Smith** is Associate Professor of Preaching and Ethics at Emory University's Candler School of Theology. He thinks theologically about the practices and institutions of American Protestantism in the season of their disestablishment. He develops thick descriptions of everyday church life that open into political theology, cultural criticism, and practical wisdom for ministry. In pursuing this project, Smith draws on theology, social theory, and the history of Christianity in the United States.

(ted.smith@emory.edu)

**C. Melissa Snarr** is Associate Dean for Academic Affairs and Associate Professor of Ethics and Society at Vanderbilt Divinity School. Prof. Snarr's research focuses on the intersection of religion, social change, and political ethics. As a Christian social ethicist, she draws on a variety of methodologies, with special concentration in sociological and political theory as well as comparative religious ethics (focusing on Islamic political thought), to understand how religion transforms the world. She teaches courses ranging from "Modern Christian Political Thought" and "Religion and Social Movements" to "Religion and War in an Age of Terror" (comparative Muslim/Christian).Dr. Snarr seeks to bridge the worlds of religious activists and academic ethicists to deepen the understanding of religious traditions and practices in order to enhance the work for justice.

(melissa.snarr@vanderbilt.edu)

**Scott Woodward** is Academic Dean at Oblate School of Theology. He has experience in religious education in school, parish, and diocese; has over 20 years of experience at OST primarily focusing on lay formation; has done extensive work in ecumenical and interreligious dialog; has experience teaching in the area of pastoral theology, including ecumenism, lay formation for ministry, Vatican II and its reception, and Church History. His research interests include ecumenical and interreligious dialog and the study of Vatican II. Current ongoing research concerns the contribution of the Archdiocese of San Antonio to Vatican II and how Vatican II affected the archdiocese.

(rsw@ost.edu)

**Amos Yong** is Dean of the School of Theology and School of Intercultural Studies and Professor of Theology and Mission at Fuller Seminary. Amos Yong came to Fuller Seminary in 2014 from Regent University School of Divinity, where he taught for nine years, serving most recently as J. Rodman Williams Professor of Theology and as dean. Prior to that, he was on the faculty at Bethel University in St. Paul, Bethany College of the Assemblies of God, and served as a pastor and worked in Social and Health Services in Vancouver, Washington. Yong's scholarship has been foundational in Pentecostal theology, interacting with both traditional theological traditions and contemporary contextual theologies—dealing with such themes as the theologies of Christian-Buddhist dialog, of disability, of hospitality, and of the mission of God. He has authored or edited almost four dozen volumes. Among the most recent is *The Future of Evangelical Theology: Soundings from the Asian American Diaspora* (IVP Academic, 2014).

(amosyong@fuller.edu)